C000256685

London's greenest architecture

The Sustainable City

Harriet Thorpe & Taran Wilkhu

HOXTON MINI PRESS

Introduction

Six ways to build a sustainable city

Live

Work

Play

Share

At Segal House in Honor Oak (p.70), architect Lizzie Fraher worked closely with the homeowners on their self-built extension, using off-the-shelf materials to ensure minimal wastage and creating space for a green roof, which both provides the family with more access to nature and helps regulate the building's temperature.

How can a city be sustainable?

Cities hold the key to our sustainable future on Earth. For, at this moment in time, cities present both a pressing problem, and a potentially world-changing solution. On the one hand, cities currently account for about 70 percent of global carbon emissions and consume over 60 percent of global resources – even though they occupy just 3 percent of the world's surface. Their population density creates a need for high-rises and skyscrapers, which have traditionally relied on carbon-guzzling concrete and steel for their construction. And their unchecked expansion is causing environmental problems that, due to our globalised world, reach far beyond their urban limits – resulting in global warming and climate change.

On the other hand, cities create an unparalleled opportunity to share resources, allowing a more efficient use of the things that take a huge toll on our environment – from transport, to food, to heating. Because of this, city-dwellers actually tend to have lower individual carbon footprints than their rural counterparts. And their population density also has its benefits: the compact living inherent in cities can help to prevent urban sprawl and keep the countryside green, as it should be. Add to that convenient commutes, expansive social networks, exciting economic opportunities and manifold cultural activities, and it's not hard to see the appeal of city life.

Perhaps this is why, nowadays, most of us – just over half of the world's population – live in cities and why, with the global population rising, urban living is on a steady upwards climb. In Europe, the city-dwelling statistic is even higher: 75 percent and counting. And around the world, more and more megacities (those with a population of more than 10 million) are evolving. In short, cities are here to stay, and they will continue to expand, so if we are to unlock a greener future, ensuring they are built and operated more sustainably is an increasingly urgent task. Imagine the difference we could make if we were to drastically reduce that 70 percent of global carbon emissions cities account for. Which brings us to the question: what exactly is a sustainable city?

First off, a sustainable city should provide all the basic and necessary provisions for the people who live in it, including safe resources, services and affordable housing. At the same time, it must present dynamic opportunities, shared prosperity, social stability and make environmentally friendly living an easy choice for its citizens. A well-designed city should not make us feel guilty or confused about sustainability, nor present it as a luxury only available to a few. A sustainable city should repair, enhance and contribute to the regenerative health of our Earth. It should make good environmental decisions on behalf of its inhabitants, and promote a better quality of life for us and the natural ecosystem – because the two are intrinsically connected.

Many of the problems with our cities today stem from how they are built. Together, the architecture and construction industries are responsible for nearly 40 percent of the world's carbon emissions, in part due to the material resources and energy that they use. But there is hope: architects can improve this figure through design. The day-to-day energy consumption of buildings can be reduced – whether that's by upgrading an old building, or developing a new, low-energy one. Carbon-sequestering natural materials can replace concrete and steel. And buildings can be creatively re-used instead of being demolished, to reduce waste and save resources.

So, why have we chosen to focus on London? Well, besides the fact that we live in and love this city, we believe that London – one of the top five richest cities in the world, with a population that's set to reach 10 million by 2040 – has a global responsibility to lead by example as a sustainable city. And in many ways, it is. Look to its traffic congestion charge and 'Ultra-Low Emission Zone' tackling vehicle pollution, its bicycle-sharing schemes, efficient public transport system, and the 3,000 parks across the city. In fact, in 2019, Londoners were reported to have the lowest carbon footprint in the UK. And, while the wider UK has set a goal to reach carbon neutrality by 2050, London Mayor Sadiq Khan is more ambitiously aiming for 2030.

London's progressive reputation as a city of intelligence, innovation and ideas is upheld by the people who live here, and it's their vision of a sustainable city that we present in this book. Across the collaborative discipline of city-making outlined in these pages, you'll meet architects and designers with solutions that break boundaries, who are full of ambition and endless compassion: from iconic pioneers (such as Sarah Wigglesworth, p.82, and Haworth Tompkins, p.156) to savvy new voices (like PUP Architects, p.232, and Surman Weston, p.182). Plus, you'll meet many non-architects who are part of the process – people who have committed their investment, vision, curiosity, time, open-mindedness and trust to make each piece of the city more sustainable.

That being said, London's architects and designers still face some serious challenges. Energy is being wasted across the capital on heating badly insulated and draughty buildings and, as a result, the most recent statistics show that 398,000 London households live in 'fuel poverty' – meaning that spending what's required on their fuel costs would leave them with an average income below the poverty line. The capital also generates vast amounts of waste (seven million tonnes each year). Its green spaces may be numerous, but they vary greatly in accessibility (for people) and quality (for plants and animals). Meanwhile, 16 percent of major roads in London still exceed the legal limits for nitrogen dioxide, one of the main contributors to air pollution. All of these issues have a knock-on effect on people's health across the city: life expectancy differs by up to 19 years between boroughs, with the largest disparity between some of the richest and poorest people in the UK.

It seems clear, then, that in London, as in cities in general, we have both a compelling problem and a wealth of hopeful, exciting solutions. Some of London's buildings have been pioneering low-energy design for decades, while other newly built projects represent fresh innovation in the field – in some cases, taking it to extremes. Architect Justin Bere's house (p.24), for example, uses the natural energy of the climate for heating and cooling, pushing energy use down to a minimum. The BedZED housing development in Sutton (p.52) reaches near zero-emission living with an innovative use of solar panels and a heating system fuelled by plant-based biomass. A timber school canteen in south London (p.206) is thermodynamically-designed for natural cooling, reducing energy demand and keeping air fresh. While clever community buildings across the West End (p.218), Fulham (p.224) and Surrey Quays (p.232) use simple energy-saving ideas such as thick insulation to cut energy bills for councils and communities.

Elsewhere in London, architects are designing buildings that prioritise reuse and recycling to reduce waste. Statistics from 2018 show that, in the UK, 62 percent of waste is made up of construction debris, so the capital city is tasked with innovating to improve that figure: buildings and materials are being repurposed at all scales, from a colossal concrete council office once destined for demolition that's been transformed into a hotel (p.174), to a house renovation that employs its own construction waste as part of its new design (p.42). Additionally, London architects are designing buildings that can be easily deconstructed and rebuilt elsewhere in the future as the city evolves, such as a flat-pack farm in Waterloo (p.110) that takes waste out of the equation entirely. They're also channelling building materials away from carbon-intensive concrete and steel, and in their place suggesting powerful alternatives in natural materials – from timber to cork to stone – that store carbon, instead.

But, as well as being low carbon and low energy, the buildings in our city have a social responsibility far beyond their four walls – to enhance the lives of Londoners. Through good design, architects can create cities that promote a healthy social ecosystem of living, working, playing and sharing in sustainable, collaborative, joyful ways. Examples of this include encouraging walking and cycling to keep us healthier (see N Family Club, p.196); preserving cultural heritage that helps us to feel personally invested in the buildings around us (see Gasholders, p.76); collaborating closely with communities to make people feel heard and empowered (see Belarusian Memorial Chapel, p.188); and helping preserve green spaces that Londoners (both humans and wildlife) can enjoy together (see Phoenix Garden Community Building, p.218). A building designed to enhance people's lives, which in turn becomes loved and cared for, will have far more longevity, encouraging repair and renewal rather than an endless cycle of demolition and waste.

Importantly, all of the sustainable projects in this book are intimately connected to their distinctive London context – whether to the climate, the history or the community. They are optimistic buildings that reimagine the type of city that London could be. As much as this book is about architecture, it's about people, too – those working together to design the city, and those thriving within it. Could you be a part of the sustainable development of your city? Look around you: what works, what doesn't and, crucially, why? The challenge from here on is to create action, transforming cities into places where we can connect and collaborate in a way that benefits not just ourselves, but also, crucially, the planet. We hope that the pioneering projects in this book will inspire and galvanise you to help your city become that world-changing solution – whether you live in London or beyond.

Harriet Thorpe
London, March 2022

Six ways to build a sustainable city

Architecture faces a pressing challenge: it needs to help urban centres do less damage to our planet. But where do we start? Here are six big ideas that could form the building blocks of better cities.

1. Go beyond carbon-neutral

Calculating a building's carbon footprint can help to reduce its impact, both in its design and its day-to-day operation – but to achieve true, holistic sustainability, we need to look at a wider picture than emissions alone.

How do buildings emit carbon?

The carbon emissions of a building can be broadly divided into two categories: the carbon it takes to build it (embodied carbon), and the carbon the building emits during its lifetime (operational carbon). Architects can help to reduce carbon emissions in both these areas. For instance, a low-embodied-carbon building could be built from renewable, natural materials (such as timber), or make use of an existing building. A low-operational-carbon building is one that can function with minimal energy – for example, by being designed to heat and cool passively (see p.16).

But do carbon emissions tell the whole story?

Today, technology makes it possible to calculate the carbon emissions of each material used to design a building, and the ongoing carbon impact the building will have on the environment. That means architects can actively reduce the carbon consumption of buildings by looking at these numbers. However, numbers don't tell the full story. No matter how low the carbon emissions of a building, if it is empty, unused or even unloved, it is fundamentally unsustainable. The equation for sustainable architecture needs to also take into account factors that are harder to measure than carbon emissions – such as how much a community's love for a building can extend its lifespan.

A carbon-negative future

High carbon, low carbon, zero carbon – what about negative carbon? Instead of *consuming* high amounts of carbon, could buildings actually help to absorb carbon from the atmosphere? Well, what if they were built solely from natural materials that sequester carbon when they grow, or ran on self-generated renewable energy? Or made room for essential, carbon-absorbing greenery? These are just some of the myriad, innovative ways that architects can aim for carbon negativity.

BedZED (p.52), a pioneering eco-village in south London, considers sustainability from all angles. It is built with natural and recycled materials, but it also creates its own energy, makes space for greenery and empowers its inhabitants to live a sustainable lifestyle with ease.

2. Build with timber

Think of a city, and you might picture an expanse of concrete and steel – but could there be timber skyscrapers in the sustainable cities of the future?

What's so good about wood?

With the help of modern technology, wood is now a more versatile building material than ever before. And, because trees absorb carbon when they grow, any amount of timber used in a building can reduce its carbon footprint. Wood should always be sourced sustainably, so that the trees it came from are guaranteed to be replanted at the same rate they're felled. Plus, when it comes to the construction site, timber structures can be erected much more quickly than their concrete and steel equivalents and create cleaner, quieter building sites.

What's the problem with steel and concrete?

Together, steel and concrete are responsible for around 15 percent of global emissions of carbon dioxide. And cement, the main ingredient in concrete, is made in an intensive process that adds 2.5 billion tonnes of carbon dioxide to the atmosphere each year and consumes almost 10 percent of the world's industrial water supplies. In cities, where concrete is used intensively, it traps heat and pollution, raising the average air temperature (which is known as the 'heat island effect'). While architects can *limit* the use of concrete and steel – and ensure that they are used for the longest amount of time possible and then recycled – a better solution lies in replacing them with more sustainable alternatives, such as timber!

Building tall with timber

Can you believe that some types of timber are stronger than steel? Modern manufacturers have been able to strengthen wood for use in construction by slicing it into thin pieces, then layering it up and binding it with a treatment, so that it becomes extremely durable, reliable and fire-resistant. Today, engineered timber can be used for the structure of buildings up to 18 storeys high – imagine what might be possible in future.

The structure of Ibstock Place School Refectory (p.206) is made up of a diamond-shaped lattice of engineered timber, which is filled in with slatted oak panels. As well as sequestering carbon, all of these timber pieces were cut to length at manufacture, reducing pollution and waste.

3. Use what's already there

Lots of buildings already exist. Some of them are not very energy-efficient, while others just don't seem all that useful anymore. But that doesn't mean we need to demolish them: instead, we need to *rethink* them.

Seeing worth, not waste

What if we were to treat all existing buildings and materials as precious? When we change the way we think about reuse, design starts from the resources surrounding us. In response to the environmental need to reuse buildings, many architects are starting to treat ordinary buildings as artefacts, elevating them into characterful contributions to the city by upgrading them with new designs.

How can old architecture fit new purposes?

Old buildings can be given totally new purposes via clever and considered redesigns. A warehouse can become an office. An office block can become a hotel. For architects, the first step in this process is to complete an in-depth evaluation of a building, assessing its strengths and weaknesses. Then, they must decide how to reshape it – preserving where possible, and replacing where necessary. The problem with many old buildings is that they are wasting energy on heating due to bad insulation and drafts, but retrofitting a building (updating it with new systems or structural elements that were not part of its original design) can improve its energy efficiency and reduce its environmental impact. In fact, properly insulating a (previously badly insulated) building can reduce its heating demand by up to 80 percent.

Designing out waste

Today, there's a growing movement among architects to design buildings that can be easily re-used in future. There are a few different ways to achieve this: buildings intended for permanent use can be 'future-proofed' through design – for example, with flexible floor plans and durable materials; or more temporary architecture can be designed specifically for reuse, so that the structure has multiple 'lives' – it might use flat-packed parts that can be deconstructed, stored and rebuilt elsewhere.

The Standard hotel in King's Cross (p.174) was once an office building. To convert it, the architects re-used 94 percent of the original building, while equipping it with modern sustainable features such as water and heat recycling systems.

4. Make buildings self-sufficient

Buildings should be designed to warm and cool 'passively' – by harnessing the power of the energy that surrounds them, like the sun, the wind and even the heat of our appliances.

What is passive design?

Passive design principles draw on an understanding of climate and the natural qualities of materials to keep a building at a comfortable temperature inside all year round, without needing to rely on fossil fuels. Many of these principles have been used for centuries in architecture – way before we had radiators and air conditioning – and often, they mean designing a building in reaction to its surrounding conditions, such as the prevailing weather.

How do we put passive design into practice?

Being able to open a window in your house to cool it down in summer is a form of passive cooling. Being able to open two windows on different sides of your house to cross-ventilate, is another (more effective) form of passive cooling. But, what if you were at work, in a glass skyscraper, on the 10th floor? If you couldn't open the window, you would probably just turn on the air conditioning, ultimately using up fossil fuels. This example barely scratches the surface of how passive vs. mechanical methods can control the temperature of a building. Many passive methods are invisible and designed into the fabric of the building itself, such as thick insulation or airtightness. There are many simple, passive measures that can go a long way in reducing your energy bills.

The Passive House Standard

Some architects and engineers are particularly interested in how passive design principles can work together to achieve a building that has the lowest possible heating demand. The Passive House Standard sets out guidance and a series of targets that need to be met in order for a building to reach that goal. When a design ticks all the boxes, it can be officially labelled a 'Passive House', which is an internationally recognised concept.

Architect Justin Bere tends to beehives on the green roof of his low energy house, The Muse in Islington (p.24), which puts many passive design principles into practice.

5. Make it (actually) greener

Cities shouldn't only serve humans: they need to work for entire ecosystems. Architects can promote the wellbeing of plants and animals by planning in biodiverse green spaces.

How do design and nature interact?

Green spaces in cities must be designed so nature can thrive alongside humans. Architects can carve out space for nature in cities: from planning green roofs, balconies and gardens into buildings; to designing taller buildings that create population density and leave green space green. Landscape architects, meanwhile, work specifically on the design of green space itself. They make sure a city's parks and commons are optimised for humans (for example, with wide, accessible pathways that are well-lit at dusk for safety, or benches for people to eat their lunch on), but they should also make green spaces work for nature – incorporating protected areas for animals and plants to flourish.

What's biodiversity and why do cities need it?

When an ecosystem is more diverse, it stays in better balance – local animals, plants and microorganisms can depend on each other to flourish. When the variety of creatures and plants present have the right conditions to thrive in the ecosystem, that's biodiversity. In the past, cities and the countryside have felt like polar opposites: grey vs. green. But, since cities are expanding to meet the demands of the growing global population and using up more land, they have an increasingly important responsibility to support ecosystems, instead of just pushing them away beyond the city limits.

How do you make a city green?

There's plenty landscape architects can do to make sure cities have their share of nature – whether that's making space for plants to grow wild, creating habitats for wildlife, or planting trees in dense 'mini forests', proven to increase biodiversity. And it's not just architects who can make a difference – you could plant a native species in your garden, or (if you don't have your own outdoor space) campaign for more tree-planting in your local area.

Landscape architect Paul Gazerwitz surveys his work at Omved Gardens in Highgate (p.150). His design for this green space included dense, native planting for biodiversity, and a new water drainage system and pond to encourage wildlife and prevent flooding.

6. Create places people care about

When architecture enhances our wellbeing, we are more likely to care about it and consequently take care of it – keeping it well-maintained and protected from the threat of demolition.

How can architects encourage 'care'?

When a building is deeply connected to the needs, hearts and history of its community, it can encourage pride, respect, ongoing maintenance and consequential longevity. Architects can create this deep connection through good design. It starts with thorough research on the area – responding to, or preserving, history and culture. By listening to the community, even inviting them to be part of the design process, architects can inspire inhabitants to have a sense of ownership over their city. In addition, architects can anticipate the long life of a building, using materials that are durable, or easily replaceable, and easy to maintain. They could even supply a maintenance manual, to make it easier for owners and users to keep their building in good health.

Why does caring matter?

Though buildings and cities are large and seemingly invincible, they aren't much different to other objects that we use on a daily basis. A building's materials require maintenance, especially when they are being used a lot. Just like the objects we use in daily life, if we care for our buildings, they will serve us better and last for longer – allowing us to pass them down to future generations.

Whose responsibility is it to care for a city?

From city mayors to local councillors, building owners to building users, residents to visitors, everybody has a responsibility to care for the city. In this book, you'll meet plenty of people who are not in the architecture industry, but have become part of the design process. They have helped to make the innovative, sustainable ideas of architects a reality. Through their care, investment, vision, ambition, curiosity, time, open-mindedness, trust and collaboration, our city is a better place. Take their action as your inspiration.

At the Belarusian Memorial Chapel in Finchley (p.188), architect Tszwai So (pictured left) created an authentic, meaningful space by collaborating closely with London's Belarusian community – including Dr Karalina Matskevich, leader of the Francis Skaryna Belarusian Library (pictured right).

Live

Clever homes are central to a sustainable life in the city. From low-energy and Passive Houses to timber high-rises, resourceful renovations and self-builds, we can all pioneer environmental change from home.

A 'passive' house that actively works with nature

THE MUSE, ISLINGTON
ARCHITECT: JUSTIN BERE
BUILT: 2002

Architect Justin Bere's home and office in Newington Green is one of London's most iconic low-energy houses. A hidden fortress with layered roof gardens tucked behind a terrace of four Grade I-listed houses, the house uses passive design principles to keep it warm and cool, working in symbiosis with nature in the heart of the city.

Growing up in cold houses in Ireland and Somerset, Bere was acutely aware of how warmth is integral to living happily and comfortably at home. Rather than relying on radiators to blast out ever-escaping heat, he wanted to design homes that could stay warm using insulation and the natural qualities of the sun, thereby avoiding the need for central heating.

His own house in London provided a perfect test-bed for these low-energy design ideas. The building has thick masonry brick-work, triple-glazed windows, and is sealed as tightly as possible to stop heat escaping and drafts entering. Because of the transparency and thinness of glass, windows are the places where heat is gained and lost at the highest rate in a building. Wanting the house to be filled with daylight, Bere chose the best quality triple glazing to minimise heat loss in winter, and designed shading systems to keep the interior cool in summer.

The floor plan and windows closely correspond to the path of the sun. The open-plan kitchen and living room are positioned on the first floor, which benefits from the most natural

'The Passive House Standard doesn't need to be a design straitjacket. It just shows you the environmental implications of your decisions. It is a bit of a discipline.'

JUSTIN BERE, ARCHITECT AND FOUNDER OF BERE:ARCHITECTS (PICTURED BELOW)

daylight and warmth. Here, there is a large east-facing window and south-facing glazed doors that open up onto a roof garden filled with plants, flowers and a pond. To the west, high-level clerestory windows run the length of the living space, catching the warmth of the winter sun as it sets, with bespoke blinds preventing excessive afternoon heat in summer.

The rest of the house was planned around this key living space. The bedrooms are on the ground floor where it is quietest and also coolest in summer, and a large study sits on the second floor, which also benefits from lots of light.

Passive design makes the most of tools and methods that work with nature to make buildings feel comfortable inside. The approach stems from the Passive House Standard, an official design certification established in Germany that measures and qualifies the extent to which a building can be labelled as low energy or 'passive'. Although this house was designed several years before Bere learnt about Passive Houses, it nevertheless aligns closely to it. Now, he uses it as a design method for most of the houses that he works on.

While the Passive House qualifications are stringent, here Bere shows how the design principles can be followed in creative ways. 'The Passive House Standard doesn't need to be a design straitjacket,' he explains. 'It just shows you the environmental implications of your decisions. It is a bit of a discipline. For example, if you want to design a building with a less efficient shape, you need to compromise with more insulation.'

Bere's house is full of character, as well as energy-saving ideas. His love of Scandinavian design can be seen in the warm, timber-lined interiors, while his love of nature shines in the green roofs, tended with a light touch to encourage wildness. He even keeps bees to make honey for his family and friends. Ultimately, Bere's desire to build a sustainable house in the city was about finding a home where he could feel happy and in balance with nature. 'You don't need to compromise on good design to build a really efficient, low-energy home.'

Inside Bere's home, reclaimed timber wall panelling, timber cabinetry and his collection of landscape paintings give the space a warm and natural interior atmosphere.

KILL YOUR TV
BAKE CAKE DRINK TEA
PLAY A KAZOO
choose handmade love your town
SING KEEP IT WONKY
BARTER & SWAP
MAKE STUFF
WRITE LETTERS
CHAMPION THE UNDERDOG
GROW YOUR COMMUNITY
LOVE ALL THE PEOPLE
LIVE YOUR LIFE
AARDVARK
BE KIND
FLOWER GUIDE

Building with a joyful, natural material: cork

CORK HOUSE, LEWISHAM
ARCHITECTS: NIMTIM ARCHITECTS
BUILT: 2019

At this terraced Victorian house in south London, cork takes a leading role in an extension and renovation built for a creative couple and their two children. As well as being a sustainable choice as a natural material, cork proved to be a remarkable multi-tasker, reducing the need for additional materials. Here, it performs as a rainproof cladding on the new extension, a highly effective insulator, and an interior wall surface with great acoustic properties.

Cork is a renewable material that stores carbon as it grows and is fully compostable. To make it into a building material, bark is cut from the cork-oak tree every nine years, then compressed into granules and made into building blocks, which can be used in many different ways. For this extension, Nimtim Architects built a blockwork wall, then layered the cork blocks either side, leaving the cork exposed on the exterior and interior. The architects didn't need to add any other materials, such as further cladding or insulation, plasterboard or even paint, which are all commonly used in housing projects.

'If a material is durable and fit for purpose, why clad over or cover it – why not let it be expressive and celebrate it?' suggests architect and co-founder of the practice, Nimi Attanayake. She often works with families looking to renovate and extend their existing homes, and always encourages her clients to consider new uses of sustainable materials. 'When researching a concept for a client, we feed sustainable materials into the design from the get-go, so the ethos of sustainability is embedded,' she explains. 'Then, when presenting different material options to clients, we try to empower them to make bold, unorthodox decisions.'

For Attanayake, using sustainable materials in new contexts is an exciting process of discovery and collaboration with material suppliers, other architects and clients who are often keen to be involved. 'We never take a cookie-cutter approach and never do the same thing twice. There is an element of embracing the unknown when trying out new materials, but we give them that life to take on, and then we return, to see how the material is settling into its environment.'

As well as the functional and sustainable properties of cork, Attanayake liked its earthy texture and colour, which matched the hues of the Victorian brickwork. To this palette, the architects added a slick, bright salmon-pink window and pivot door frame, and a cool-grey resin floor for the interior. Together, the combination of colours and materials creates a playful, contemporary space reflective of the family's identity. Returning to the house, Attanayake notes that the shade of the cork has become richer, although it still smells just as woody and toasty – and she hears it has excellent acoustics for big family parties.

Family by family, Attanayake and her team are creating warm, joyful and more energy-efficient homes across the city. 'We often work on period properties that are not really fit for modern life anymore,' she says. Though much-loved architecturally, many of London's Victorian houses haven't changed very much since the advent of running water at the turn of the 20th century. Nimtim is aiming to bring them into the 21st century: 'We scenario-test, future-proof, upgrade and adapt these houses into flexible places for families to live in for another 100 years.'

'If a material is durable and fit for purpose, why clad over or cover it – why not let it be expressive and celebrate it?'

NIMI ATTANAYAKE, ARCHITECT AND CO-FOUNDER OF NIMTIM ARCHITECTS (PICTURED RIGHT)

The ground floor extension features a wide pivot door framing views to the garden, and a glazed roof light bringing daylight deep into the interior. The cork blocks that clad both the exterior and interior walls provide natural insulation and rain protection.

2 MARCH
2012
THE GARETH LOCKRANE SEPTET
Saul Bass
CHIP KIDD
667-999
334-666
001-333

London's first timber high-rise

MURRAY GROVE, HOXTON
ARCHITECTS: WAUGH THISTLETON ARCHITECTS
BUILT: 2009

When this timber residential building was constructed in 2009, it was the tallest of its kind in the UK and Europe. Rising nine storeys with 29 apartments, it showcased the possibilities of wood in the design of tall buildings, rather than the more common structural materials of concrete and steel. If you walked past it in the street, you wouldn't know it had a timber structure, nor would you be able to see that by choosing this material, the embodied carbon emissions of the building have been reduced by 60 percent.

'The world is becoming increasingly urban, so when it comes to sustainable design, the challenge is high-density housing,' says Andrew Waugh, cofounding director of Waugh Thistleton, an architectural practice that is focused on making large-scale impact with sustainable design. His approach to sustainability has always been to make change at the broadest level: 'It's in the mainstream where you can make a real difference.'

Waugh's building design required three trees for each person living there – and for every tree used in the structure, one was replanted. Wood, in its engineered form of cross-laminated timber (CLT), was used for the majority of the design, from the load-bearing structure to the floor slabs, stairs and lift cores. Timber sections of the building were pre-fabricated at manufacture, then assembled around the central axis in a honeycomb-like formation. The construction was much quicker, cleaner, quieter and healthier for

> 'When it comes to sustainable design, the challenge is high-density housing. It's in the mainstream where you can make a real difference.'
>
> ANDREW WAUGH, ARCHITECT AND CO-FOUNDING DIRECTOR OF WAUGH THISTLETON ARCHITECTS (PICTURED BELOW)

construction workers and the community than a concrete and steel alternative would have been. Thanks to the prefabricated elements, there were 80 percent less deliveries, which reduced pollution and material waste on site. The building went up in just 49 weeks, with the structure itself taking only 27 days, having been built by four workers, each working a three-day week.

When you look at the building, you might be able to sense the efficiency and simplicity of its design, even though you can't see its internal structure. With evenly shaped and spaced windows, and inset balconies, the overall aesthetic is one of thoughtful restraint. It has a softer presence in the city than its concrete or masonry counterparts, subtly reflecting back rather than imposing on its surroundings. The lightweight wood-pulp and cement-panel cladding, for example, are arranged in a geometric grayscale pattern based upon the natural dappled shade that hits the building.

For Waugh, who has lived in Hoxton since he was 24 years old, the outward appearance of the building wasn't necessarily a priority. 'When designing sustainably, the decision process that you go through needs to be about material efficiency,' he explains. 'Beholden on us all is a level of modesty about everything that we do from now on: no more excess. And it's the same in architecture as it is in any other walk of life.'

The load-bearing structure of the nine-storey building is made of cross-laminated timber. These timber sections were pre-fabricated at manufacture, and assembled around a central axis in a honeycomb-like formation.

A home where sustainability feels playful

MOUNTAIN VIEW, SYDENHAM
ARCHITECTS: CAN
COMPLETED: 2020

'"Waste not, want not" was a phrase my grandmother used to say in the kitchen about food,' says architect Mat Barnes. This old adage is now memorialised on the tiled steps leading into his own kitchen. It inspired his design approach to the renovation and extension of a once-derelict Edwardian semi-detached house in Sydenham, experimenting with materials otherwise destined for waste, and using them in highly crafted and unexpected ways.

From the street, the two-storey red-brick looks like any other house on the terrace. Yet, take a few steps inside, and you'll realise it is anything but ordinary. From the entrance hall, the floor drops down by one metre into an open-plan kitchen and dining room, with an airy 3.4-metre ceiling height. Here, a bright blue, white and grey kitchen, a red-painted exposed steel structure and a textured concrete-effect wall collide to create a theatrical interior. The partially demolished former exterior wall has been left in place as a natural room divider, separating the light-filled living space, which overlooks the garden through colossal floor-to-ceiling glazing.

Barnes liked the craggy outline of the half-knocked-down brick wall, as a reminder of the building's past. 'I stripped back the layers of the house and assessed what was there already, then used those layers to bring character,' he says. 'I always tell clients to pause and wait until we can make design decisions on site, because we often find something worth using. Instead of covering up materials from the past,

‘I stripped back the layers of the house and assessed what was there already, then used those layers to bring character.’

MAT BARNES, ARCHITECT AND FOUNDER OF CAN (PICTURED RIGHT)

we can use the texture that is already there as part of the design.’

This resourceful mindset can be seen throughout the house. In the kitchen, the colourful countertops and cupboard doors are made from a terrazzo of recycled plastic chopping boards and milk-bottle tops. The cabinets and legs of the dining table are made from the rubber of recycled tyres, while the bench cushion is made of recycled foam, salvaged from discarded seating. The living room wall is decorated with fragments of broken plaster moulds, which the local plasterer donated for free, rather than throwing them away.

‘In an age of scarce resources, it won’t always be sustainable for a whole building to be made of one specific material,’ says Barnes. ‘As architects, we need to be adaptable to what materials are available. Naturally, that might give a less singular and more collage-like aesthetic. There might be a lot going on, but this can also start a new aesthetic – one that evokes a sense of the surreal.’

Instead of relying on finite natural resources, Barnes suggests that we have fun ‘faking it’ instead. Here, playful layers of material treatments often disguise what is beneath. The old fireplace, which he found in the house and reinstated, has been sprayed with a stone-effect paint. Elsewhere, the once-tired wooden dining chairs have been sprayed with a crackle-effect paint, completely transforming their character.

‘You can’t be too stringent on the final result,’ says Barnes. ‘The design should emerge from what’s already there on site.’ It’s through this savvy and organic process that a new, highly personal home has emerged from the rubble of an old one. Barnes’ irreverent approach to design is perhaps best exemplified by the strangest bit of the house – a recycled aluminium mountain (inspired by his favourite Disneyland ride) that sits atop the new extension, and gives Mountain View its name. In all, the house is a brilliant example of how creative reuse, repurposing and the adaptation of materials can be the building blocks for a whole new vision.

Architect Mat Barnes, founder of CAN, pictured at home in the new extension of his Edwardian semi-detached house.

Barnes used to work at McDonalds and found his illuminated golden arches on eBay. The messaging on his tiled kitchen steps, meanwhile, was inspired by the thriftiness of his grandmother.

An estate built to reduce energy bills

AGAR GROVE, CAMDEN
ARCHITECTS: MAE, HAWKINS BROWN, ARCHITYPE
ENGINEERS: MAX FORDHAM
BUILT: 2018 – ONGOING

Our individual carbon footprints can be reduced simply by living in a city with public transport and local shared facilities. Yet, in a city such as London, lowering that carbon footprint is not a priority for everyone. And it shouldn't have to be: the government and local councils should be taking on the responsibility, on behalf of all of us. Here, in the borough of Camden, the council has taken steps to do exactly that, equipping its residents with a housing estate designed to reduce their carbon footprints and energy bills.

Complete with gardens, playgrounds and sports areas, this modern estate replaces a set of poor quality, low-rise, 1960s residential buildings. The demolition of these buildings was carefully considered by the council and the community, who decided that starting afresh with new homes that were larger, more comfortable and more energy-efficient than their predecessors would be more sustainable in the long term. The construction was phased in six stages. Only one social tenant moved away from the estate and all the other tenants were gradually rehomed as the buildings were finished.

The design of the new homes was a collaboration between three architecture practices – Mae, Hawkins Brown and Architype – who worked with Max Fordham engineers to make sure that all of the buildings were as energy-efficient as possible. Engineers Hero Bennett (pictured left of image, with Michelle Christensen, Senior Development

'When you move into a Passive House after you have lived in a draughty 1960s building, you discover that it works in a different way.'

KATIE CLEMENCE-JACKSON, PARTNER AND SENIOR ENGINEER AT MAX FORDHAM

Manager at Camden Council, centre) and Katie Clemence-Jackson (right) of Max Fordham achieved this by following the stringent design guidelines of the Passive House Standard: a certification that sets out how architecture can use materials and the natural climate to create the most comfortable interior temperature, thereby requiring the lowest energy demand possible. For example, there are high levels of insulation and airtightness to create a consistent temperature inside. The buildings are oriented north-south-facing where possible to capture the most sun throughout the day, with dual-aspect windows in each home for cross ventilation. These interventions, among several other passive design techniques, resulted in a 70 percent reduction in energy demand compared to the previous homes on the estate.

After the first residents moved into the first phase of completed buildings, Camden Council led a survey to find out what people thought of their new homes. Clemence-Jackson and Bennett spoke to individual residents to ask them about interior temperatures, fresh air, comfort and other aspects of the development, such as the gardens.

'One of the things people really noticed was that air quality had improved,' says Clemence-Jackson. 'When you move into a Passive House after you have lived in a draughty 1960s building, you discover that it works in a different way. There are no draughts, making for very comfortable conditions. Fewer sources of heat are needed because the homes are so well-insulated and airtight, and you can open windows without it becoming too cold. People also really appreciated the generously sized balconies.'

Importantly, these design measures are not just about saving energy: they are also crucially about comfort – creating warm, healthy homes in which people can live their lives. Dual- and triple-aspect buildings are ideal for ventilation and cooling, and they also connect people to the outdoors, bringing in daylight and views of their neighbourhood. Every resident now has either a garden, balcony or terrace, whereas previously no one had any private outdoor space. In addition, there are communal play areas and plots for growing vegetables. Ultimately, Agar Grove's approach to sustainability creates the best value over the whole lifetime of the buildings.

Many of the homes in the estate have unique floorplans, and are often arranged across split levels, plus each has either its own balcony, terrace or garden.

13

An eco-village that empowers its residents

BEDZED, SUTTON
ARCHITECTS: ZEDFACTORY,
IN COLLABORATION WITH
BIOREGIONAL AND PEABODY GROUP
BUILT: 2002

In the suburbs of London, the Beddington Zero Energy Development (BedZED) is a colourful, eco-friendly village with 100 homes, an office, a school and a field. The experimental development was initiated by Bioregional, a charity and social enterprise focused on sustainability, which was co-founded by environmentalist and social entrepreneur, Sue Riddlestone OBE. The vision was for an ambitious zero-carbon community, where the Bioregional office could be based, its goals could be put into practice and being sustainable could become achievable for all residents.

Bioregional teamed up with architect Bill Dunster, founder of ZEDfactory (an architecture practice specialising in low-carbon building) and London housing association, Peabody, to design and build the village. Together, they considered sustainability across every aspect, from locating the site near public transport connections to the materials used and how they would be constructed, to the day-to-day running of the community, including its energy use and reducing the carbon footprint of every person living there.

BedZED's eight rows of interlocking buildings, roof gardens, pedestrian bridges and pathways have a utopian feel, with their colourful window frames and air cowls. Just over half of the materials used to build the village were sourced within a 35-mile radius, reducing the carbon costs of transporting the heavy materials. Fifteen percent of the materials were also reclaimed or recycled –

‘People think of sustainability as an add-on, but it needs to be incorporated into design thinking from the beginning.’

SUE RIDDLESTONE OBE, CO-FOUNDER OF BIOREGIONAL (PICTURED RIGHT)

for example, most of the steel was reclaimed from refurbishment work at Brighton Railway Station. The timber cladding is made from green oak harvested from woodlands in nearby Croydon and Kent.

The architectural design was driven by renewable solutions to heating and cooling, achieved through high levels of insulation, airtightness, passive solar heating and photovoltaic panels. Heating is also controlled ‘passively’ by the architecture as much as possible. Arranged in east-to-west rows, the homes have south-facing double-glazed windows woven with photovoltaic (solar) panels that catch the energy of the sun. On the other façades, windows are much smaller and are triple-glazed to prevent heat loss, while a much thicker than average 300mm layer of rock wool insulates the walls, ground-level floors and roof.

The brightly coloured rooftop cowls rotate on vanes to face the wind, collecting fresh air and expelling stale air, which travels in and out of the homes through vents. In winter, a heat exchanger warms incoming fresh air with the heat of the outgoing air. In summer, the cowls catch the breeze to bring cooler air in and windows on different sides of the homes can be opened for cross-ventilation.

In addition to these passive and renewable measures, BedZED has a small-scale ‘district heating’ network that circulates hot water around the village through a network of insulated pipes to each home’s hot water tank, which is more energy-efficient than every home having its own boiler. The water is heated by a biomass boiler that burns wood pellets, a near zero-carbon fuel, while electricity is purchased from the grid on a green tariff. After a little experimentation over the years, the eco-village is now close to fulfilling its original zero-carbon ambition.

Although these energy-saving measures were designed to reduce the impact of the village on the environment, they were also created to empower its residents: to reduce their energy bills and enable them to be more in control of their own carbon footprint. ‘A zero-carbon building was our brief to the architects, but what we brought to BedZED was zero-carbon sustainable living in a very holistic way, designed from the perspective of a user,’ says Riddlestone. ‘People think of sustainability as an add-on, but it needs to be incorporated into design thinking from the beginning.’

BedZED makes sustainable living – from energy-saving, to composting and growing, and to car-sharing and bike-storing – easy. ‘Nobody wakes up in the morning and thinks, “Oh, I want to go out and destroy the planet,” but that’s how much of society is set up,’ Riddlestone continues. ‘Life needs to be made easy for us to make the right decisions – to look for the good and reward the good.’

Many homes at BedZED have conservatories or 'sunspaces' behind the south-facing windows. Double-glazed windows and doors separate these spaces from the rest of the home, which can then be opened and closed to control the interior temperature.

HELIOS ROAD
Bioregional

SCARPA

A low-cost timber house in a pub yard

STRANGE HOUSE, DEPTFORD
ARCHITECTS: HUGH STRANGE ARCHITECTS
BUILT: 2010

Tucked behind a terrace of houses in Deptford, this single-storey, two-bedroom house is built in a disused pub yard. From his ground floor flat, architect Hugh Strange had looked out onto the scruffy piece of land and imagined a serene, sustainable house where he could live with his young family, while converting his flat into an office for his architecture practice with a timber extension (pictured left). He made his live/work dream a reality by designing a simple, low-cost timber house in the yard. The set-up served him well for over ten years, until he recently moved out in search of more space for his growing family.

The yard has been transformed, through very economic means, into a calm urban oasis. The 75-square-metre house is hidden by an old brick wall covered in climbing ivy, and is built atop an old concrete slab found on the site. Because the house is so lightweight, foundations didn't need to be excavated: instead, Strange simply added a smooth layer of concrete to the existing slab, which was then polished up and left exposed as the interior floor.

A light-coloured, cross-laminated timber was used for the majority of the house. The fast-growing spruce wood was sustainably grown in Switzerland, where it was 'cross-laminated' for extra strength and durability, and prefabricated into the exact-sized pieces needed for the walls, partitions and roof of the house. Once they reached the site, the timber structure was constructed in less than a week.

To ensure an airtight, non-draughty design, lots of insulation was added to effectively seal the house. Windows were carefully placed to allow daylight in, without too much heat gain. An exhaust air heat pump supplies underfloor heating and hot water, and the roof is covered in solar panels, reducing the need for energy from the grid.

For Strange, the house was a test-bed for developing his own architectural language. He sees particular promise in timber as a low-cost, low-carbon, sustainable building material. 'Cross-laminated timber has the potential to replace much of the use of concrete, masonry and steel as a major building material, with huge carbon benefits to it,' he explains. 'Instead of burning carbon and releasing it into the environment, like the production of steel and concrete, timber actually captures carbon.'

In addition to the pale, cross-laminated timber, which is finished with white hard wax oil, Strange also used a darker-coloured tropical hardwood from Nicaragua for the doors, window frames and interior furniture. On first look, it's a controversial choice – hardwoods take much longer to grow and, in the tropics, illegal logging has caused the deforestation of valuable habitats.

'It wouldn't usually be sustainable to use this kind of wood,' says Strange, 'but there was a hurricane in Nicaragua and the supplier was able to collect the timber off the ground, and certify the wood as FSC-sourced. I describe it as the fairtrade argument. If you're confident that you're supporting a socially and environmentally responsible business outside the First World, then I think there is a strong ethical basis and a good sustainability case for this strategy.'

Strange's balanced approach to sustainable design brings many different ideas together under one roof, from the reuse of a neglected urban site, to the cross-laminated timber structure, and the passive and renewable approaches to energy use. The house also enabled him to live a more sustainable life in the city, reducing his commute down to a short stroll across a courtyard, enabling him to better connect with his family and nature.

The walls, partitions and roof of Strange's house are made from prefabricated panels of FSC-certified spruce, while the window frames, doors, cupboards and built-in furniture are all made from sustainable tropical hardwood, which he sourced from a company based in Central America that collects wood from trees felled by hurricanes.

'The house is in a densely urban and busy part of London, yet we still tried to find balance with nature. Instead of being a house with a garden, it feels like you're almost living in the garden.'

HUGH STRANGE, ARCHITECT AND FOUNDER OF HUGH STRANGE ARCHITECTS (PICTURED LEFT)

The pioneering home of an engineering icon

MAX FORDHAM HOUSE, CAMDEN
ARCHITECTS: BERE:ARCHITECTS
ENGINEERS: MAX FORDHAM
BUILT: 2019

This three-storey, three-bedroom mews house in Camden was the home of Max Fordham (1933–2022), a leading engineer instrumental in designing sustainable buildings around the world. While architects design how a building should look, engineers work out how to make it possible, honing in on technical elements, and ensuring the comfort and quality of the interior, from daylight to acoustics.

Fordham founded his practice in 1966, bringing together mechanical, electrical and environmental engineering, with a focus on low-carbon and low-energy design. He was always interested in the connection between buildings and the environment, the effects of nature and the climate, and the impact of the heat that we create as humans living in homes.

It was a privilege to be able to photograph Fordham in his home in the summer of 2021, before he passed away in January 2022. Built in the back garden of his former residence, a Victorian terrace on Camden Square, the house was designed by Fordham with architect Justin Bere (whose own home is featured on p.24) and engineer Ali Shaw. The building was a very personal project, which brought together many of Fordham's ideas on sustainability, amassed through his life's work.

The leading idea was to eliminate the need for heating, instead using materials and design to harness waste heat from household appliances (such as the fridge, television and lights) and human bodies, plus the heat of the sun, to create a comfortable interior temperature all year round. Designed to meet the Passive House Standard, a certification for low-energy architecture, it has triple-glazed windows and is five times more insulated and draught-proof than your average building. These measures mean that the house stays warm and comfortable without central heating.

Here, the word 'housewarming' is taken quite literally. When Fordham moved in, he had a housewarming party – warming up the house to 24 degrees celsius through the heat of the guests. Because the house is so well insulated, the heat simply stays inside the house, unless you open all of the windows.

In order to be a well-functioning modern house, the design also required good ventilation and a way to heat water. To ensure a healthy flow of air, mechanical ventilation works with a heat exchanger that preserves an optimum interior temperature, while moving stale air out and fresh air in. For hot water, a heat pump is located within a sun trap; for efficiency, it's programmed to heat 24 hours' worth of hot water in the mid-afternoon, when the air temperature outside the house is warmest. Solar panels are also installed on the roof to contribute to this.

While eliminating heating was always the main incentive, for this house to be truly sustainable, it had to also be an uplifting and happy place to live. 'The most energy efficient house would have no windows – but daylight is so important for wellbeing,' says engineer Shaw. And so, instead of eliminating windows (which during the night typically lose ten times more heat than a wall), Fordham designed insulated window shutters that automatically close at sunset, then reopen at sunrise to benefit from the natural light and heat of the sun.

Recently awarded the accolade of being the UK's first net-zero carbon home by the UK Green Building Council, Max Fordham House shows how a material-and-energy-efficient building can also be beautiful place to live. There is humanity in its practicality and sustainability: the covered entranceway for storage makes city life flow more easily, the cork flooring is warm underfoot, and the little garden that wraps around the house, together with the planted balcony terraces and green roofs all prove good for the soul, as well as for the environment.

'To me, sustainability means creating a part of the city that contributes towards a zero-carbon, biodiverse and brighter tomorrow.'

ALI SHAW, ENGINEER AT MAX FORDHAM ENGINEERS
(PICTURED LEFT OF IMAGE)

Max Fordham (centre) pictured with his son,
Jason Fordham (right), and engineer Ali Shaw, in 2021.

A minimalist self-build extension

SEGAL HOUSE, HONOR OAK
ARCHITECTS: FRAHER & FINDLAY, IN COLLABORATION WITH CÉLINE DALCHER WILKHU
COMPLETED: 2019

In the leafy Honor Oak neighbourhood of south London, an '80s home has been extended and refurbished, while staying true to the self-build house movement pioneered by its original architect, Walter Segal (1907–1985). Segal designed modular houses, using timber and off-the-shelf materials that could be assembled by anyone with a set of tools, which meant that they could also be repaired, extended and upgraded by anyone, too, thereby totally liberating the homeowner.

Taking the same hands-on approach, Lizzie Fraher, architect and founder of local practice Fraher & Findlay, worked closely with homeowner Céline Dalcher Wilkhu, an exhibition designer, to create their streamlined extension. Dalcher Wilkhu and her husband, Taran Wilkhu (an architecture and design photographer, who photographed all of the projects in this book), wanted a creative office space and a spare room, which could also double up as a den for their two sons. Plus, as with every growing family, more storage was high on the requirements list.

Throughout the process, Fraher and Dalcher Wilkhu continued to ask themselves: 'What would Walter do?' They selected readily available building materials from the local DIY store: black corrugated metal sheets to clad the timber frame; exposed spruce plywood panels for the walls; and oriented strand board (OSB), made of compacted, criss-crossing strands of wood, for the in-built storage.

'A house is a liability and its owners have a long-term responsibility to take care of it. This design makes that ongoing relationship easy to manage.'

LIZZIE FRAHER, ARCHITECT AND FOUNDER OF FRAHER & FINDLAY (PICTURED RIGHT)

'These materials are cost-effective because they are mass-produced, which means waste is minimised as they are efficiently sourced and made,' notes Fraher. 'Off-the-shelf materials are also easy to assemble, install and repair: a house is a liability and its owners have a long-term responsibility to take care of it. This design makes that ongoing relationship easy to manage, so the lifespan of the house can be prolonged.'

In addition to materials, the space itself is economically designed to ensure that every inch is functional. The wedge-shaped extension isn't large – and only broadens to two metres at its widest – but it is very clever. Making use of the sloping land that the house sits on, it drops down one level to create room for a home office that is connected to the garden, and tucks the spare room/den beneath the existing house. A new plywood staircase is lined with useful storage, and the repositioning of the front door in the extension means that there is more space in the open-plan kitchen and dining area.

As Dalcher Wilkhu was involved in the design and construction process, she was able to reuse and rehome existing materials around the house. A window from the old entrance was repurposed as a kitchen cabinet door. A box of leftover tiles from a previous bathroom renovation found a spot in the new part of the kitchen. She describes the process as 'organic' and likes how the reused elements carry memories of the house and its evolution.

As an exhibition designer, Dalcher Wilkhu is always reimagining spaces and building sets. At home, she is the same, collecting and storing objects and materials for that opportune moment when they might be used to reset the stage. 'We would all like to live more minimal lives, but as humans we love stuff; we like to collect things,' she says. 'For us as a family, it's all about having good storage in every room. But, instead of buying a new cupboard, we build storage in every wasted space in the house, like under the stairs – all you need is a void and some shelving.'

Her favourite part of the house, though, is a little less tangible. What she loves most, she says, is the daylight that floods through the large window in the living space, uplifting her every day. The design of the extension enhances the flow of the house from room to room, allowing her to notice the light more and more, as she looks out at the wildflowers on the extension's green roof and across her neighbours' self-builds to the city beyond.

Building upon the house's original design by architect Walter Segal, the materials for the extension had to be affordable, readily available and require no skilled labour to assemble.

Luxury homes born from an industrial past

GASHOLDERS, KING'S CROSS
ARCHITECTS: WILKINSON EYRE
BUILT: 2017

Soaring, circular-steel gasholders – or gasometers – were once commonplace in the British landscape, providing heat and power to homes and cities from the 19th century onwards. Hulking relics of the 'town gas' era (when gas was produced by burning coal in ovens), these monumental structures have slowly disappeared, following the discovery of natural gas under the North Sea in 1965 and the subsequent development of National Grid pipelines.

In King's Cross, three Grade II listed, cast-iron gasholders – originally built in 1867 and revered for their craft and technology – have found renewed modern purpose as epic frames for low-energy luxury homes. Three circular buildings have been slotted into the centre of each gasholder. Each building reaches a different height in reference to the movement of the original telescopic drums that would rise and fall as the pressure of the gas inside fluctuated.

We had the pleasure of a tour of the complex with its architect, Chris Wilkinson (1945–2021), in 2019 – at which time he was also living in one of the flats here. Wilkinson was of the belief that architecture is the bridge between art and science – a philosophy apparent at the Gasholders, which is both visually poetic and environmentally high-tech, as well as at the redevelopment of London's Battersea Power Station, another famous and much-loved piece of the city's industrial heritage that Wilkinson worked on.

The residential buildings at the Gasholders are highly insulated and airtight, with

‘We wanted to retain the presence of the structure, but give it new meaning and use for the future. Working with circular geometry has resulted in really beautiful ideas. What began as a challenge turned out to be a blessing.’

CHRIS WILKINSON (1945–2021), ARCHITECT AND FOUNDING DIRECTOR OF WILKINSON EYRE (PICTURED BELOW)

triple glazing; the wedge-shaped apartments have expanses of windows for natural light, yet recessed balconies and sliding perforated shutters to prevent overheating. These, as well as other design measures, have resulted in a 45 percent reduction in operational carbon in comparison to an average UK home. Additionally, programmable devices in each home record and display energy usage, encouraging efficiency.

The gasholders are protected by Historic England, which is why they had to be painstakingly restored and refurbished for modern use. The 123 iron columns weighing between 6.5 and 8 tonnes were dismantled, transported to a warehouse in Yorkshire, stripped of 32 layers of paint, stress-tested, and then blasted with copper slag, before finally being transported back to London and reassembled as part of the new design.

Redefining these redundant pieces of energy infrastructure as luxury homes was quite a leap. The design wasn’t the most direct route to making a sustainable residential building. Yet, its success lies in the pride, labour and precision of restoration that resulted in the transformation of a less-than-sustainable past into something of value for the future.

Inside the structure, shared interior spaces conceived by Jonathan Tuckey Design combine stained oak timber panels with brushed stainless steel and brass finishes. Meanwhile, on the roof terrace, landscape architects Dan Pearson Studio selected robust and low-maintenance plants such as ornamental grasses creating an informal, natural-feeling garden for residents.

9/10

How to live off-grid in the city

STRAW BALE HOUSE, ISLINGTON
ARCHITECTS:
SARAH WIGGLESWORTH ARCHITECTS
BUILT: 2001

Architect Sarah Wigglesworth's experimental house was designed as a test-bed for eco-friendly architectural ideas. The aim was to make the house as low carbon and self-sufficient as possible using an array of techniques and features, from passive design to natural building materials and a vegetable garden. Today, the house – and its adjoining office for Wigglesworth's architectural practice – still stands up to the strength of its original design, yet it's recently undergone an eco-upgrade, using new technology to better insulate and reduce the building's energy use.

'The whole agenda was about trying to create a new model for sustainable living in an urban environment,' says Wigglesworth. 'When we started designing in 1995, "green" buildings were what hippies did and the idea of living a sustainable life in a city seemed to be a bit alien. But I'm from the city, I'm born and bred in Islington and I wanted a model that could work on my patch.'

The house uses readily available, low-tech materials, many of which are waste products, easily recycled, bio-degradable and low carbon. Yet these materials are all used in highly technical ways. For example, straw bales, after which the house is nicknamed, provide excellent insulation. Procured from a barley harvest in 1997, the 550 bales are protected by a transparent polycarbonate plastic rain screen, with a layer of perforated metal and insect mesh to keep them both dry and ventilated. Elsewhere, sandbags, railway sleepers, recycled concrete-filled gabion baskets and even quilted-fabric cladding have, perhaps surprisingly, stood the test of time as effective building materials.

Each façade of the house is treated differently, according to its orientation and relationship to the sun, so that the exterior of the building can passively control the temperature of the interior as much as possible. In addition, the building employs techniques that were used to heat and cool houses before the arrival of cheap energy. Based on thermodynamic and aerodynamic science, manually operated, shuttered air-vents on the ground floor allow air in, which rises through the house, to a tower that draws air out. 'The building is very interactive,' notes Wigglesworth. 'It acts like a layer of clothing that you can take off or put on, depending on how you feel – allowing you to be in complete control of your own environment.'

The almond-shaped larder in the kitchen uses similar technology, harking back to a pre-fridge era. It draws cool air from beneath the building and keeps the temperature low thanks to thick brick walls. 'Larders were previously designed in a cool part of the house, usually facing north on an outside wall,' explains Wigglesworth.'Yet, since the advent of cheap energy, we have lost the knowledge of these traditional ways of designing.' Other parts of the house encourage more sustainable ways of living, too. The productive vegetable garden, for example, is accompanied by an easy access ground floor utility room to make storing tools and cleaning up after gardening easier. Similarly to larders, utility rooms have disappeared from the design of many urban homes today.

After 20 years in the house, Wigglesworth decided to retrofit the building to improve its sustainable credentials even further. Following a thorough analysis using technology such as thermal imaging, she increased insulation and improved air-tightness to keep the temperature as constant as possible inside. Among other updates and tweaks, external shading was added over the large windows to keep the building cooler during the summer months. These changes resulted in a 62 percent reduction in heating demand.

By learning from the past and responding to advances in research and technology, Wigglesworth's experimental house has given her first-hand experience of innovations in sustainable design, many of them her own. She applies these experiences to her wider work, in buildings such as care homes, schools and residential buildings.

'The building is very interactive: it acts like a layer of clothing that you can take off or put on, depending on how you feel.'

SARAH WIGGLESWORTH, ARCHITECT AND FOUNDER OF SARAH WIGGLESWORTH ARCHITECTS (PICTURED RIGHT)

The office wing (pictured opposite) is clad with quilted fabric and sandbags, which provide a great acoustic buffer from the adjacent train track. Recycled concrete-filled gabion baskets are used to clad the steel structure below, limiting the use of new concrete.

Many inventive building materials clad this sustainable fortress, which is surrounded by a productive kitchen garden and an assortment of trees. The tower holds a library and a little snug at its apex, while the dining room (pictured opposite) doubles up as a conference room and connects to Wigglesworth's office.

Turning a historic yellow building green

GREAT ARTHUR HOUSE, CLERKENWELL
ARCHITECTS: JOHN ROBERTSON ARCHITECTS
COMPLETED: 2019

A 20th-century beacon of modern city living, Great Arthur House is a 15-storey residential building at the heart of the Golden Lane Estate, one of London's most influential post-war housing estates. Originally designed by Chamberlin Powell & Bon in the 1950s, the architecture was cutting edge for its time: the pioneering high-rise employed steel-reinforced concrete and a curtain wall made of glass, aluminium and teak. It later became Grade II listed for its heritage value.

The magnificent sunshine-yellow building is admired by many and loved by residents for its light-filled interiors and views across the city. However, unfortunately, like many ageing residential buildings in London, it suffered from leaking windows, draughts and poor insulation, resulting in high energy bills.

'Great Arthur House has existed for 60 years already and our brief was to extend it for another 60 years,' says architect John Robertson, who was faced with the challenge of retrofitting the building while preserving its protected design, including its distinctive roof, which features a decorative concrete 'sun-scoop'. 'In many ways, heritage conservation aligns well with sustainability. When you work with an existing building, you're starting from a good position because around 70 percent of a building's carbon emissions exist in its structure and fabric. So, if you can keep refurbishing and extending its life, you'll have a much greater efficiency for the carbon already used.'

Although the concrete structure is resilient enough to last longer than 100 years, the curtain wall, which keeps the structure dry, is not so durable. Despite being highly technical for its time, it was flawed when it came to energy conservation: like many old buildings, it had no insulation. Today, architects understand the importance of double glazing and insulation to keep residents warm, as well as the all-important thermal bridging to prevent condensation.

Robertson and his team set about designing a new curtain wall that was an exact – but more sustainable – replica of the original in order to reduce the building's energy use. They used the same materials of glass and aluminium, but this time, they were recycled. The windows are now double-glazed and mineral-wool insulation has been added, resulting in a 31 percent reduction in heat loss. The thickness of the new wall was increased, yet the proportions and style of the original curtain wall were painstakingly preserved: even the yellow-coloured glass was matched and sourced from the original manufacturer, Pilkington.

'As an architect, I always think you should leave a building or a city in a better way to the way you found it – by vastly improving energy consumption, but not compromising the character of a design, or altering its DNA,' says Roberston, who has transformed many listed buildings in London, respectfully preserving them while improving their sustainability. 'This is one of the biggest challenges facing British housing at the moment – how to make existing homes more energy-efficient and upgrade them in a sensitive way.'

'As an architect, I always think you should leave a building or a city in a better way than how you found it.'

JOHN ROBERTSON, ARCHITECT AND FOUNDER OF JOHN ROBERTSON ARCHITECTS (PICTURED RIGHT OF IMAGE)

Architect John Robertson (right) pictured with Ed Marchand, a resident of Great Arthur House.

Each flat here comprises a bedroom, living room, kitchen and bathroom, with a small terrace. They were designed for single people and couples, including nurses and policemen who had to live near to their work in the city.

Work

Sustainable workplaces should serve the environment and the economy. As an international centre of innovation, London needs flexible, hybrid office spaces that are practical, daylight-filled, and mindful of their emissions.

Modern co-working in an old warehouse

FORA WORKSPACE, SPITALFIELDS
ARCHITECTS: PIERCY & COMPANY
COMPLETED: 2019

In the late 17th century, Spitalfields was established as a centre for the silk industry by the French Huguenots, who built houses with large interiors for looms, high ceilings for fresh air and light-flooded attics for weavers to work in – many of which you can still see around the neighbourhood. Somewhere along the line, our modern workspaces lost many of these attributes, which even though we aren't now working at large looms, are still very important to our wellbeing.

On Princelet Street, architects Piercy & Company saw potential for a high-ceilinged, mid-19th-century warehouse to be adapted into a modern co-working space. Their aim was to retain as much of the existing building as possible (its old brick walls, timber joists and steel structure), saving huge amounts of carbon through reuse, thereby reducing the pollution and waste from demolition and reconstruction.

The design looks to the future as much as it preserves the past, equipping the building with a new lease of life. The entrance, where a horse and cart would have once pulled in, is now a double-height lobby with a smart reception desk. A sculptural red staircase slices through the centre of the building, climbing up to a daylight-filled two-storey extension. Interiors welcome all types of working styles, from solitary focus in private nooks, to informal collaboration in the stepped forum-style event space.

'Most of the buildings knocked down today in London are '70s and '80s offices, built when people didn't understand workspaces,' says

Stuart Piercy, architect and founder of Piercy & Company. 'They weren't built for wellbeing: floor-to-ceiling heights are low, windows are small, façades are skinny and there is no quality of space. Most of the good, old buildings you can retain, especially light-filled industrial buildings, which have large ceiling heights.'

Here, despite the expansive ceiling heights, daylight was still limited, as the deep building is part of a terrace in a densely packed neighbourhood. To counteract this, the new extension includes a sawtooth roof with lots of windows to maximise natural light, just like the Huguenot attics. If the high-performance, solar-controlled glazing, which stops too much heat from the sun entering, had been invented in the 17th century, no doubt the Huguenots would have chosen this, too.

'Resilience is really important to us as architects,' says Piercy. 'If buildings are good, they can adapt. We always try to design with four different uses in mind, so our buildings can be resilient to future unknowns. I think the most unsustainable building is one that is not used, or not used well. You've got to build for the behavioural changes that might happen.'

What would the Victorians think if they saw their warehouses being adapted into contemporary offices? And, how different might east London look today if we had repurposed more of these buildings, instead of knocking them down? Through a process that Piercy describes as 'stitching' together old and new, this particular warehouse has the resilience to serve yet another wave of industry in Spitalfields – and many more to come.

Aiming to preserve as much of the original building as possible, the architects conducted a forensic investigation of the warehouse, including a full 3D scan that they could study from the studio. Working within the old structure, they added many modern finishes, including built-in storage joinery, timber flooring, terracotta sinks, terrazzo surfaces, and the distinctive central staircase.

'I think the most unsustainable building is one that is not used, or not used well. You've got to build for the behavioural changes that might happen.'

STUART PIERCY, ARCHITECT AND FOUNDING DIRECTOR OF PIERCY & COMPANY (PICTURED BELOW)

In a city as dense as London, outdoor space is very important to wellbeing at work. To bring this into the design of the Fora workspace, the new roof extension was carefully set back to make room for an outdoor terrace, adding vital access to fresh air while preserving the character of the original building when viewed from the street.

A recyclable, self-built garden studio

MANBEY POD, STRATFORD
ARCHITECT: U-BUILD / STUDIO BARK
BUILT: 2019

In the garden of a terraced house in Stratford sits a neat timber studio, built from a flat-pack kit that was delivered to the door. Homeowner Peter Thompson built the studio, with some help from his brother, for his wife, Joan Keating, a talented quilt-maker. Customised to its plot, with a large picture window to the world, the studio was designed by U-Build, an off-shoot of Studio Bark's architectural practice. Studio Bark set up U-Build to simplify timber architecture and create an accessible design system that would be straightforward, low-energy, efficient, fully recyclable and that could be constructed by anyone, anywhere.

U-Build connects the dots between DIY, construction and architecture. The building system of modular birch-plywood boxes multitasks as both the building's structural support and a shell for sheep's-wool insulation. After being assembled to a custom design, the building was clad in textural western red cedar panels to keep it dry. The pieces of timber that make up the modular boxes are digitally designed to fit within a standard-sized piece of plywood and cut with a CNC machine, keeping waste to a minimum. Packaged at the factory, with all the connecting elements included, the studio can be built using just a mallet and a drill.

For Thompson and Keating, this was a practical and fortuitous choice for their garden studio. They had seen a U-Build community centre in their area, and had admired its design and concept. They needed a structure that could fit through their narrow front door and that could also be carried all the way through the house – the only way to access the garden. They also really liked the idea that it could be deconstructed and rebuilt elsewhere if they moved. Equipped with an average set of DIY skills, Thompson was up for the challenge and ultimately found the process far more rewarding than he had anticipated: gaining a new understanding of how ventilation, sunlight and insulation can work together to heat and cool a building, as well as the satisfaction that comes with completing a self-build project.

Crafting a better understanding of architecture is integral to Studio Bark's approach. 'We want people to be involved in the creation of their environment, so they can have an appreciation for it,' says Tom Bennett, an architect at the practice. They host construction workshops for architecture students, in order to foster more sustainable attitudes towards the use and value of materials in the industry. They also want to make construction accessible: when you build something yourself, the idea of repairing, adapting or extending the space starts to feel less daunting.

'We need to get to a place where everything is environmentally thought through,' says Bennett, on Studio Bark's empowering approach to sustainable design. 'Sustainability is about doing no harm, but we should really be aiming for design that actively contributes to the environment in a positive way. Designing in a regenerative way is about creating real benefits to ecosystems, as well as people, so we can allow the world to heal a little bit.'

'We want people to be involved in the creation of their environment, so they can have an appreciation for it.'

TOM BENNETT, ARCHITECT AT STUDIO BARK
(PICTURED OPPOSITE)

Peter Thompson (pictured above) built the studio for his wife, Joan Keating, using a colour-coded instruction manual. Keating (pictured right) now uses the studio to work on her characterful quilts.

STOP
CLIMATE
CHANGE

A flat-pack architects' office in a city farm

OASIS FARM, WATERLOO
ARCHITECTS: FEILDEN FOWLES
BUILT: 2014

Adjacent to the train tracks of London's busiest station, you might be surprised to discover a thriving little farm. It is, in fact, somewhat of a hybrid farm-office, because its design also incorporates workspaces for three organisations – local charity Oasis Hub Waterloo, Wiltshire-based Jamie's Farm, and architectural practice Feilden Fowles. The three organisations found synergy in their social and environmental sustainability aims, and decided to pool their combined skills that cover architecture, community services, children's education, youth work and agriculture to create a unique and mutually beneficial place in the city to work.

The collective formed a plan to make use of an unused inner-city piece of land owned by the nearby Guy's and St Thomas' Hospital, which was awaiting development. Architects Feilden Fowles designed a low-rise collection of timber barns that, as well as hosting animals and gardens, combines facilities for education and work, including classrooms, a multi-purpose barn, an annexe and a studio with desk space for all three organisations.

The design was carefully considered so each enterprise could happily co-exist, while all benefiting mentally from the surrounding nature and animals at the farm: 'The layout of the farm allows both functions – education and workspace – to be quite separate day-to-day, if needed. But, working in the studio, wandering up at lunchtime to see the goats or even just taking a call in the garden can provide a welcome break. Similarly, the courtyard garden

> ‘It can flatpack into a kit of parts. Each stave is numbered, so you can take it down and put it back up again like a jigsaw.’
>
> ELEANOR HEDLEY, ARCHITECT AT FEILDEN FOWLES (PICTURED RIGHT OF IMAGE)

provides a quieter area for visiting groups to use, or a place to retreat to during events on the farm,’ says Eleanor Hedley, architect at Feilden Fowles.

She describes the architects’ approach to sustainability as ‘low-tech’. Their designs incorporate simple passive solutions, such as natural ventilation. The use of local materials, including UK-sourced Douglas fir and larch, results in a design that is low-carbon. And inspiration is taken from historic building techniques that favour economy and simplicity.

The multi-purpose barn design, for example, references the lofty ceilings of traditional tithe barns, updated for the 21st century with corrugated glass-fibre cladding around the timber frame and polycarbonate roof lights. Inside, there is an insulated classroom for 30 children, clad in galvanised steel and lined with birch-faced ply. Similarly, the studio has a solid Douglas fir frame and is clad with corrugated Onduline bitumen sheets, while the stepped, pitched-roofed animal pens are made of rough-sawn British larch.

Though nature has slowly taken over and the animals have settled in, the farm is, in fact, a flatpack. It has been designed to be disassembled and reassembled elsewhere – responding to its temporary nature on a site that will be redeveloped in the future. Assembled with mere screws and bolts, the buildings can be easily deconstructed and built elsewhere when the lease on the land is up.

‘It can flat-pack into a kit of parts,’ says Hedley. ‘Each stave is numbered, so you can take it down and put it back up again like a jigsaw. Our studio frame is modular, so it could really become anything. We did some studies to see how it could become a house, a classroom, or a different type of workspace if it was extended or divided into two smaller buildings – it is really flexible.’

The low-tech, flat-pack approach certainly doesn’t take away from the buildings’ refined aesthetic. The architects worked closely with their structural engineers and construction team to ensure beautiful craftsmanship, for a set-up that enables visitors to escape the city into a new environment. Perhaps, when it comes to building more sustainably in the city, London’s architecture could learn something from the architecture of the countryside. ‘The materials are not expensive but are used thoughtfully,’ says Hedley. ‘Agricultural buildings are already boiled down to their most practical and economic bones, so often come with this sense of simplicity and elegance.’

Nick Crane and Eleanor Hedley, architects at Feilden Fowles.

The workspaces (pictured above) are airy, uplifting and filled with daylight – north-facing clerestory windows allow light to enter with the least amount of heat gain, while hidden vents provide passive ventilation. The multi-purpose barn (pictured right) is rented out as a flexible space for events such as fundraisers, music videos, evening classes and weddings, providing revenue for the charity.

Oasis
Welcome to
Oasis Farm Waterloo

Prefab steel structures with multiple lives

THE LOW LINE, SOUTHWARK
ARCHITECTS: TDO
BUILT: 2021

How do you turn disused railway arches into modern, flexible workspaces in a sustainable way? When architects TDO were commissioned to design a replicable and reusable template to tackle the material-waste problem of short-term fit-outs, they found themselves inspired by the economy of wartime shelters. Inserting a series of part-recycled galvanised steel Nissen huts into the arches of a Victorian viaduct in Southwark has created space for a variety of businesses, including a cleaning company's logistics hub, a dance studio and an artist's workshop.

Nissen huts were invented during World War I as an economical way to make portable shelters for military use. Post-war, the structures have mainly been used for industrial and agricultural purposes. In this case, however, the half-cylindrical steel forms lent themselves perfectly to the shape of the railway arch – and provided a simple solution to insulation, waterproofing, and much more.

Steel is a material that is extremely tough and useful in architecture, although its production is energy-intensive, resulting in a high embodied-carbon status. That said, steel is easily recycled and can be recycled many times over without losing its strength: currently, about 96 percent of steel is recycled in the UK. While recycling steel is less carbon-intensive than making it anew, designing for reuse is better and skips the need to recycle altogether.

TDO's design process required close collaboration with manufacturers and careful planning. The steel that makes up the huts is supplied in standardised pieces, so the architects adapted their design accordingly; no off-cuts meant less material waste. The huts were then prefabricated at the manufacturing site, before being bolted together at the building site, meaning less construction pollution.

'Railway arches are very available in the city,' says Tom Lewith, architect and cofounding director of TDO. 'They are useful spaces for activities that might be temporary or transitory, often being leased out for a few years maximum. The structures needed to be demountable to meet that "temporary" requirement, yet we did not want them to go to waste after use. So, we designed them to be able to be broken down and refitted or stacked up, until a new arch is ready. The purpose that you see here today is just a fleeting moment in a long lifetime of use.'

Part of the temporary nature of these huts is that they 'float' inside the railway arch, without touching or attaching onto the historic brickwork. As well as the practical function of their easy deconstruction and removal, the architects were pleased that the character of the vaulted arches was preserved and could still be admired by all who stepped inside. In fact, by creating this 'space within a space', they discovered a curved void above the huts, useful for lighting, services distribution, ventilation, air circulation and even storage.

London's railway arches are often overlooked. Though they may seem uninhabitable, with their rumbling caves of leaky, cold brickwork, they are also majestic sites of ready-made architecture, providing sheltered spaces that are perfect for certain types of use (it's no coincidence that TDO have their own timber-fitted office space in a nearby arch). Increasing the density of cities in this way, by making use of every inch of existing space, also allows green spaces beyond the city to remain undeveloped.

As well as being environmentally sustainable, the workspaces are designed to be socially sustainable too, to counter gentrification. Their use of low-cost materials means cheaper rents for tenants, providing space for alternative businesses and start-ups that have been priced out of central London. With this approach, TDO shows that 'economy' does not need to mean 'basic' or 'low value'. The architects find sustainability, aesthetic appeal and optimism in the economy of materials, geometry and space. 'There is beauty in efficiency,' says Doug Hodgson, the other co-founding director of TDO. 'When using new materials and taking up space in the city, it is all about consideration and precision.'

'The purpose that you see here today is just a fleeting moment in a long lifetime of use.'

TOM LEWITH, ARCHITECT AND CO-FOUNDING DIRECTOR OF TDO (PICTURED LEFT OF IMAGE)

Tom Lewith (left) and Doug Hodgson, architects and co-founding directors of TDO.

C13 RKC

Harnessing the natural strength of stone

15 CLERKENWELL CLOSE, CLERKENWELL
ARCHITECTS: GROUPWORK + AMIN TAHA
BUILT: 2017

Near Clerkenwell Green, architecture and design studio Groupwork has designed a six-storey stone building, combining offices on the ground and basement floors with apartments on the upper levels. With its large square openings and blocky aesthetic, the imposing building looks like a futuristic ruin. Its load-bearing limestone structure feels like a surprising choice for such a large building in a capital city, yet Amin Taha, chairperson of the practice, was keen to prove the benefits of stone as a sustainable alternative to concrete and steel.

Taha has always been interested in stone as a building material, but here it felt appropriately connected to the history of the site, where an 11th-century, limestone Norman Abbey once stood. Gradually subdivided and eventually demolished in the 1970s, only a few stones of the original abbey remain, yet this new building represents a modern tribute to that past.

Taha believes that stone is a largely forgotten natural material that remains relatively unexplored in modern architecture. 'After the First World War, building was all about convenience, and concrete was emblematic of the modern age,' he explains. 'Why would you want to use stone? Stone was a material of the past. It was steel, glass and concrete that represented the future.'

While not carbon-sequestering like timber, stone is abundant, resistant and strong. 'Stone has zero embodied-carbon. The Earth's crust is made of cooled magma and sedimentary stone. It's what the entire planet is made of: we are never going to run out of stone – we have more stone than anything else. We are like termites, pulling up a bit of stone, putting it elsewhere,' says Taha. Although there are carbon emissions associated with the extraction and transportation of stone, when combined to create the structure and external finish of a building, it actually has up to 90 percent less embodied carbon than a concrete and steel building.

Due to its strength, stone can be used to support buildings potentially up to 60 storeys high. Working with engineers Webb Yates, Taha developed a post-and-lintel style design, with supporting concrete floor plates spanning eight metres from the concrete core of the building. Stone is super-resistant to fire and the elements – so much so that cladding isn't necessary and its structure can be exposed.

The façade therefore reveals the true nature of the material that supports the building. Taha left some elements with their quarry-found texture, while others were smoothed off, creating a ruin-like appearance. The limestone was sourced in France and features some beautiful details, such as swirling fossils and ammonite shells. The raw materiality of the stone becomes a beautiful part of the streetscape; it doesn't need to be overly designed, and is imbued with a sense of natural purity.

The use of stone has also inspired raw materials to be highlighted elsewhere – from the pebbled entranceway to the exposed brick of the neighbouring party wall, the simple metal staircase and the concrete flooring. In the basement office space, a floating glass meeting room elevates the working environment. The moodiness of the materials used lends itself to the bunker-like aesthetic of the basement, but roof lights in the double-height space ensure an abundance of daylight.

The interiors feel progressive, modern and architectural, reflective of the history and atmosphere of London. With this building, Taha decided to push familiar materials in new ways and alternative forms, challenging a design trajectory that some might imagine is flatlining. 15 Clerkenwell Close proves the opposite, embodying a truly contemporary approach to stone architecture.

> 'We've deliberately kept the space as stripped-down, unfinished, and unadorned as possible to keep costs and embodied-carbon low, so it feels quite raw.'
>
> AMIN TAHA, ARCHITECT AND FOUNDER OF GROUPWORK

A rooftop garden, just visible from the street, creates a space for biodiversity in the city. There are two beehives, producing honey for the residents, and the garden attracts lots of nesting birds and insects. Rainwater is collected on the roof and 90 percent of it is absorbed by the mature trees, grasses, shrubs and flowers.

> 'The Earth's crust is made of cooled magma and sedimentary stone. It's what the entire planet is made of: we are never going to run out of stone – we have more stone than anything else.'

AMIN TAHA, ARCHITECT AND FOUNDER OF GROUPWORK (PICTURED RIGHT)

Some pieces of the building's limestone were left with their rough, quarry-found texture (as pictured left), creating a ruin-like appearance, while others were smoothed off to reveal swirling fossils and ammonite shells.

Seeing the value in what's already there

YORKTON WORKSHOPS, HACKNEY
ARCHITECTS: CASSION CASTLE ARCHITECTS AND PEARSON LLOYD
COMPLETED: 2020

In Hackney, an unruly crop of dilapidated and mismatched buildings – including five former Victorian stables and a 1990s factory-style extension – has been transformed to host design studio Pearson Lloyd's offices, workshops and prototype storage. Seeing potential in the awkward two-storey complex as a canvas for bigger ideas, the designers realised that the most sustainable and low-carbon approach would be a strict retrofit, where all materials would be reused or recycled. Their aim was to equip the building with flexibility in its design, to enable a long future.

'As designers, we spend our lives repairing things: there was so much inherently good material in the building that knocking it down just didn't make sense. The decision to retrofit the old building slotted into our 20-year mindset of using materials with refinement, intelligence and care,' says Luke Pearson, designer and cofounder of Pearson Lloyd (pictured right of the image opposite, with fellow co-founder Tom Lloyd, left of image, and architect Cassion Castle, centre).

Working together with Cassion Castle Architects, the team took a disciplined approach to reuse, often embracing the oddness of the building to make the most sustainable decisions. The original concrete floor was left alone, despite its odd topography, with new flooring placed on top. The original steel structure was retained but slightly adjusted to create higher ceilings. Meanwhile crumbling brick walls were dismantled, in order to be cleaned up and rebuilt.

New materials were brought in only when absolutely necessary. A new central lobby with a bright-red steel staircase connects the two old buildings together. The insulation and environmental efficiency of the building has been vastly improved by new concrete floor slabs and roofing. A concrete ring-beam strengthened the existing Victorian structure so that it could support the new roof. In the upstairs workspace, materials bring comfort and refinement to the interior; there are pine floorboards, reclaimed from a Victorian factory in Mile End, a wood-fibre acoustic ceiling, and birch-plywood partitions and interior walls.

Interestingly, there is no air conditioning. Instead, the building is passively cooled through the careful placement of glazed openings, which encourage cross-ventilation. Meanwhile, the lobby, with its durable brick flooring, acts as a temperature buffer between indoors and out – it can be opened up in summer and closed during winter. 'We have become accustomed to devices that limit the effects of the seasons, but it is important to find a balance between the efficiency of a building and how you use it,' says Pearson.

The function of the interior spaces has been left as open-ended and non-specific as possible. In doing so, Pearson Lloyd discovered that all of their needs as a design studio could be fitted in relatively easily. Workshops for making and prototyping were suited to the industrial space, while team meetings, video calls and events felt more comfortable in the more domestic-sized Victorian stables.

Secondary to the retrofit, ensuring that the space remained flexible was a choice linked to its longevity. 'We tried to imagine not just the perfect studio for us, but also how the space would be used in 50 years' time by other people. We are guests in this building for a period of time, then there will be more guests. The quality of the crafting is part of that. If it is made well, people will look after it for longer,' Pearson explains.

This idea of future-proofing is one that can be applied across the board, from design to architecture to life. 'We have always believed that things should be designed with flexibility and neutrality,' Pearson continues. 'That doesn't mean they don't have personality, but we won't subscribe to dogma or fashion. It is a manifesto that has strangely become more and more relevant. Fashion builds in redundancy; it's built on whim and taste, and being frivolous, because it makes you feel good in the moment. With sustainability, you need to remove that layer of ego and build something that serves you for longer.'

> 'As designers, we spend our lives repairing things: there was so much inherently good material in the building that knocking it down just didn't make sense.'
>
> LUKE PEARSON, DESIGNER AND CO-FOUNDER OF PEARSON LLOYD

Luke Pearson and Tom Lloyd of architecture practice Pearson Lloyd had been based in Shoreditch for 15 years, and were seeking more space and a quieter spot. They loved the local history of Hackney Road, and wanted to join the lineage of makers and manufacturers in the area that dates back over a century.

OPEN YOUR
SHOP HERE

A temporary, vibrant use of an empty site

HACKNEY BRIDGE, HACKNEY WICK
ARCHITECTS: TURNER.WORKS
BUILT: 2021

This colourful, industrial-inspired temporary workspace sits canal-side, in an area of the Olympic Park that is slowly being developed into a new neighbourhood. The land was destined to sit empty for 12 years while the surrounding buildings were constructed, but instead this complex makes positive use of the space. In design terms, Hackney Bridge is a 'meanwhile' complex, being specifically shaped to kick-start local business and community activity, and able to be deconstructed and recycled or rebuilt elsewhere when it is no longer needed here.

The lean architecture uses minimal, low-cost and recycled materials for speed of construction and durability. Steel frames are numbered, bolted together and left exposed for ease of future disassembly. Tough industrially manufactured materials, such as corrugated steel, black timber and polycarbonate panels clad the buildings. Concrete ground slabs have been polished up and left exposed for flooring. While plywood and OSB boards, made in the UK from waste timber, finish the interiors.

With its neat zig-zag of pitched roofs, the design reflects Hackney Wick's warehouses on the other side of the canal, which are commonly used for light industry by makers and manufacturers, before coming alive in the evenings for social events. With rising rents in the area, Hackney Bridge has been created specifically to incubate small businesses, from fashion brands, to breweries, woodworkers and bakers. The five buildings offer a range

The canal-side façade of Hackney Bridge overlooks a 'mobile' community garden, which has been designed to be completely moveable, and a cycle workshop inside a recycled container.

ACKNEY
BRIDGE

of spaces, including coworking desks, studios and larger units. Additionally, to support this infrastructure, there are food kiosks, event rooms and a central public yard keeping the local ecosystem in balance and ensuring a vibrant flow of people, conversations and activities.

Hackney Bridge's architect, Carl Turner, suggests that temporary buildings could provide a more sustainable solution for an ever-evolving city. The buildings are flexible to change, while avoiding the high embodied-carbon of permanent structures and the material waste of demolition. And the low costs involved means that they are more inclusive of a variety of workers at different levels of the city's ecosystem.

'The buildings are there to create opportunity,' says Turner. 'The design is about giving the best value to the business community and empowering people. Hackney Bridge is a platform for people to make change in their lives and generate wealth. As London has become a global city, it has lost affordable workspace and that is driving people out.'

For the complex to be a success, the architectural design must be very closely connected to the day-to-day operations of the workspaces and local culture. Turner worked with developer and operator Makeshift on the project, following previous 'meanwhile' collaborations together elsewhere in London: the conversion of an old railway yard into a thriving container-city of food, drink and businesses at Pop Brixton; in Peckham, a disused multi-storey car park was transformed into an epic cultural destination, Peckham Levels.

'The simple language of the buildings forms an authentic creative environment that people can inhabit and make their own,' Turner continues. 'It's designed to not feel too "designed" – and there's always something new going on. After all, cities are constantly changing, so shouldn't everything be "meanwhile"?'

When the buildings have served their purpose at Hackney Bridge, their deconstruction plan is already in place. 'Designing for disassembly is about planning ahead, asking which parts can be recycled and sold, or if there is a new site where the building could be moved to as a whole. We have plans for every single component to be harvested at the end of this building's life,' says Turner.

While it might be sad to see the complex broken down into hundreds of pieces, its lifetime will have contributed to nurturing the wider community. Hackney Bridge is a useful test-bed for businesses to see what's needed, what's successful and what feels right. Some will get the opportunity to plug into workspaces elsewhere in the area as the permanent buildings complete, and many will have helped to define the culture that attracts new people here. So, although Hackney Bridge is 'meanwhile', the complex fits into a healthy and organic cycle of sustainable material use, as well as the greater ecosystem of the city.

'We have plans for every single component to be harvested at the end of this building's life.'

CARL TURNER, ARCHITECT AND FOUNDING DIRECTOR OF TURNER.WORKS (PICTURED OPPOSITE)

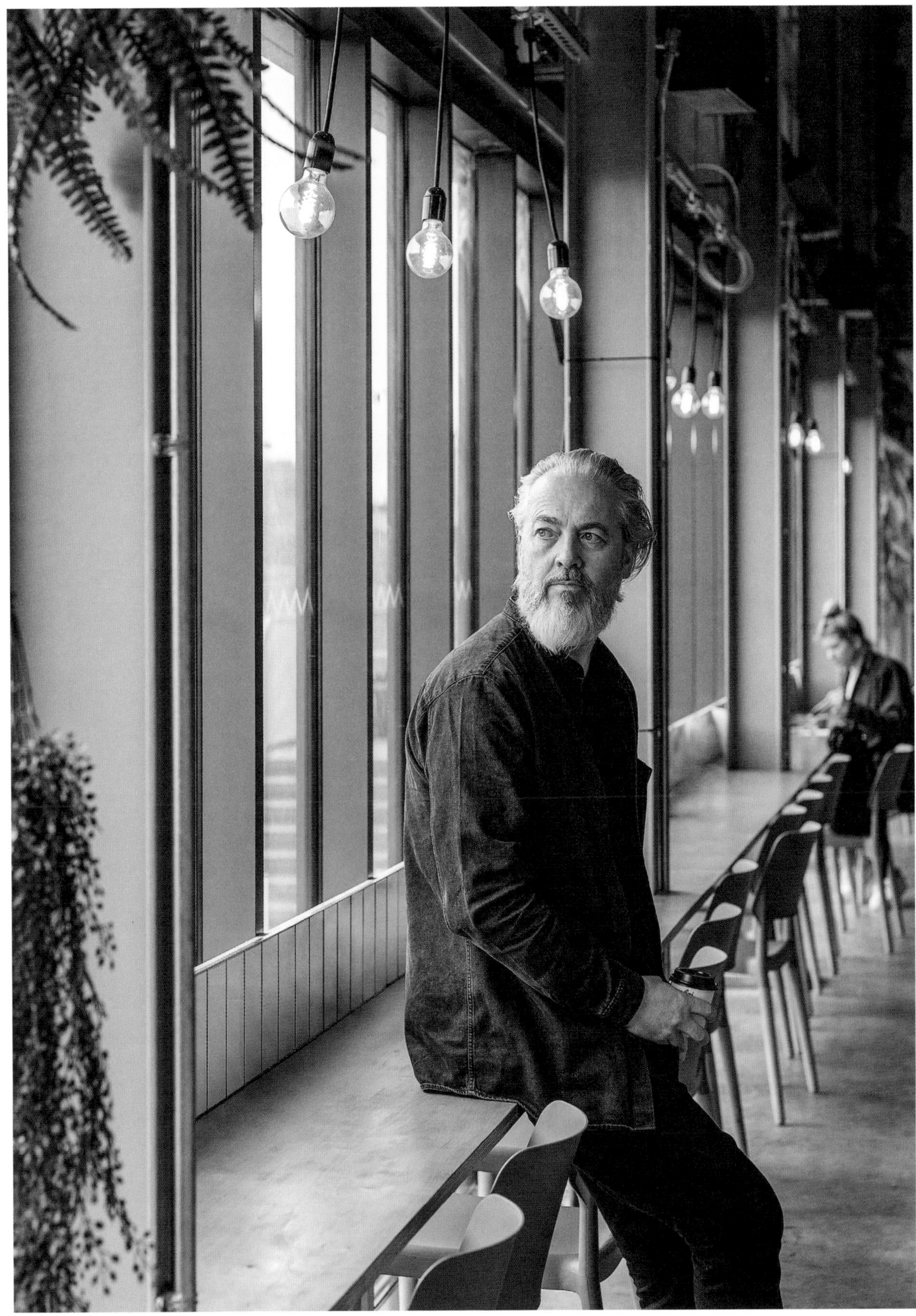

Within the complex of five buildings, work and social spaces are fused together to create a buzzy environment where everyone is welcome. There are event spaces, a market hall, small studios, maker units, a co-working space, and a corner café.

GETUP
YESTERDAY

Play

London is one of the world's cultural capitals – we like to be entertained. From playgrounds to theatres, museums to hotels, these projects show us how we can have fun in the city while creating space for heritage, nature and sustainability.

A playground designed to be loved

PARSLOES PARK PLAYGROUND, BECONTREE
DESIGNERS: YINKA ILORI STUDIO
BUILT: 2021

At Parsloes Park on the Becontree Estate in Dagenham, east London, designer Yinka Ilori OBE has transformed an out-of-use playground with a colourful design inspired by its community. The playground renewal was co-commissioned by public space experts Create London and the borough of Barking and Dagenham, as part of a series of new community structures, including street furniture made with upcycled rubble from the estate. These design interventions were all in celebration of the Becontree Centenary, marking 100 years since the first houses were built on what was touted as the 'world's largest social housing estate'.

Progressive for its time, the estate offered homes equipped with modern facilities, such as indoor toilets, bathrooms and gardens, to more than 100,000 war veterans and workers. A century later, Ilori has worked with locals to design a shared space that is reflective of the estate's history and the people who use the park today, encouraging improved local wellbeing and urban pride.

Driven by the experiences of his own British and Nigerian heritage, Ilori uses design to express the colliding cultures and diverse demographics of the city. His process starts with historical research and listening to local people. 'Communities are the fabric of the city. They breathe life into space through their stories and the legacies they leave behind. Design can give a community a voice and allow them to be seen,' he says. For this project, Ilori hosted creative workshops with residents of the estate, meeting people who have lived there for their entire lives. He also led a basketball design competition for local children.

The result is an upbeat landscape of materials and motifs that reflect the estate's unique past and present. Bespoke play-equipment includes flamingos on bouncy spring rockers: a nod to the striking pink birds that used to inhabit the park. Birdwatching and nesting structures encourage awareness of local wildlife in the park today. An old and unloved basketball court has been repainted with a vibrant pattern, totally transforming it into a destination that's very much in use. Elsewhere, concrete manhole rings have been repurposed into brightly painted urban sculptures for children to hide behind.

This joyful playground contributes to 'placemaking', a design practice that seeks to forge emotional connections between people and the built environment. When we feel inspired by and represented in our urban environment, we're more inclined to protect and care for it, helping these spaces last for a long time. Ilori's textured and functional patchwork of community memories brings colour to an otherwise grey housing estate, valuing lived experience and empowering people to take part in designing their city.

'Communities are the fabric of the city. They breathe life into space through their stories and the legacies they leave behind. Design can give a community a voice and allow them to be seen.'

YINKA ILORI OBE, DESIGNER AND FOUNDER OF YINKA ILORI STUDIO (PICTURED OPPOSITE)

The playground design encourages local pride and a sense of belonging. An old basketball court was brought to life with a new colour scheme, while new seating and rockers were inspired by the flamingoes that once inhabited an ornamental lake in Parsloes Park.

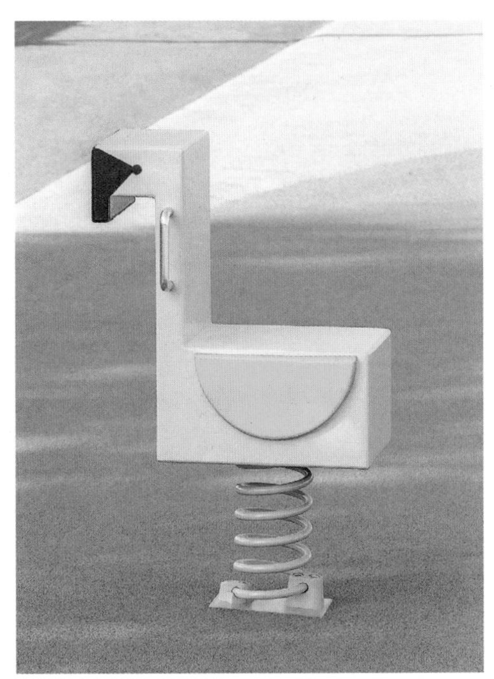

A forgotten piece of land becomes a green oasis

OMVED GARDENS, HIGHGATE
ARCHITECTS: HASA ARCHITECTS
LANDSCAPE ARCHITECTS: DEL BUONO GAZERWITZ LANDSCAPE ARCHITECTS
COMPLETED: 2017

Tucked behind Highgate High Street, this once disused site has been transformed into Omved Gardens, a centre for learning about nature, permaculture and food. Previously tarmacked, the land now hosts a 'mini forest' of nearly 300 trees, a vegetable garden and a wildflower meadow. At the top of the sloping site, an old glasshouse has been sensitively converted into a creative learning space with an interesting plywood interior structure.

Karen Pagarani, director of Omved Gardens, (pictured centre of the image opposite) wanted to create a place for Londoners to creatively and mindfully explore their relationship with the environment. She enlisted the help of architect Charlotte Harris (pictured right) and landscape architect Paul Gazerwitz (pictured left), and the trio collaborated on designing a dynamic destination for activities such as workshops, exhibitions, concerts, discussions and dinners, all centred around environmentalism.

Following Pagarani's ethos of 'treading lightly on the earth', Harris set about carefully restoring the unlisted 19th-century glasshouse – a remnant of a bygone gardening centre. Every pane of glass was removed for cleaning and was then refurbished. Where panes were broken, they were replaced with drawn horticultural glass reproducing the originals. The raw aluminium frame was painted black to protect it, and solar film was added to the roof to temper the light and heat entering on sunny days.

Functional spaces inside the glasshouse were defined by a modular landscape of birch-plywood pathways, rooms, furniture and storage. This plywood structure floats lightly inside the glasshouse, without touching the fragile shell. Each 'room' is like an island, divided by moats of plants and low timber partitions; the absence of walls redefines our expectations of an interior, encouraging a more communal, respectful and thoughtful use of space.

The glasshouse seeks to connect both people and architecture to nature. Boundaries between indoors and out are blurred by immersive views of green leaves and blue skies. Large plywood doors roll back to fully open up one side of the glasshouse to the garden. Rainwater is collected from the roof and guided through rills (water channels) down the sloping garden to a retention lake, which pools pleasantly at the bottom of the land. Collecting rainwater prevents flooding in the city, can be used to water plants during dry periods, and encourages biodiversity by attracting water-loving plant species and providing a water source for wildlife.

In the gardens, Gazerwitz was inspired by the 'mini forest' movement, based upon the work of botanist Akira Miyawaki, which proves that very dense, biodiverse planting – even on a small plot of land – is more effective at capturing carbon and improving air quality. With that in mind, the team planted an array of species, including birch, hazel and beech trees, along with plenty of shrubs, wildflowers and bulbs. Meanwhile, any concrete and tarmac was broken up and crushed to be reused as a base for pathways, and any unhealthy trees were cleared and chipped to be used for mulching. The landscape was given the urgent care and maintenance that it needed, in order to invite nature back in and allow the earth to breathe again.

Omved Gardens shows how a forgotten and tricky piece of urban landscape can become a valuable environmental, educational and creative asset. It suggests a new 'typology' of leisure for city dwellers: a visit provides an elegant interaction with nature, which combines the experience we might expect from visiting an art gallery with the learning of skills from attending a workshop, combined with the tastes of visiting a farm-to-table restaurant. Altogether, it's a place that leaves us feeling culturally and environmentally nourished.

'As architects, we are committed to raising people's understanding of sustainability.'

CHARLOTTE HARRIS, ARCHITECT AND CO-DIRECTOR OF HASA ARCHITECTS (PICTURED OPPOSITE)

OPEN AIR THEATRE
openairtheatre.com
0844 826 4242
Returns
Sales
Collections
Ticket Holders

A timber theatre nestled in the trees

REGENT'S PARK OPEN AIR THEATRE
ARCHITECTS: HAWORTH TOMPKINS
COMPLETED: 2012

London's parks are much more than green spaces that break up the urban landscape: they are also cultural destinations in their own right. Regent's Park, located between the affluent neighbourhoods of Primrose Hill and Marylebone, is home to the Open Air Theatre, which was first established in 1932. In 1976, the theatre received a significant update, when architects Howell, Killick, Partridge & Amis built the iconic, steeply raked stand with 1,240 seats. The magical theatre architecture sits gently within the park, completely surrounded by nature.

Architects Haworth Tompkins picked up the baton for the 21st century, and have been working with the theatre for over 20 years to improve and modernise the design. Speaking to the green setting, the architects wanted any new additions to be sustainable, lightweight and aligned with the existing natural environment. For that reason, timber made sense as a building material for the structure and cladding of the box office and backstage buildings, which have been placed carefully to follow the curved pathway of the park's inner circle.

The construction of the prefabricated, cross-laminated, low-carbon timber buildings was clean and fast; they went up in just three weeks, which fitted comfortably into the time available between theatre seasons. Given their lightness, the frames required minimal foundations, which meant that the established tree-root systems of the park could be preserved.

'Everything we did was lean,' says architect Ken Okonkwo. 'The majority of the design is timber, which contributed to the narrative of the site, but also meant we were able to be as pared back as possible.'

Inside the buildings, the timber panels have been left exposed, reducing the need for additional materials, while the exteriors have been clad in rough-sawn, unfinished and dark-stained larch boarding.

The design and materiality of the buildings echoes the rhythmic layering of the surrounding trees, ensuring that the architecture feels at one with the landscape. Elsewhere, planted trellises and woven-hazel façades wrap around the auditorium, creating a sheltered promenade. Another cross-laminated building, designed by Reed Watts Architects in 2018, was added in to complement the growing theatre campus.

Regent's Park Open Air Theatre challenges people's expectations of architecture in the city and suggests how it could work more successfully in tune with nature. 'The biggest task for architects today is changing the whole story of how we engage with the built environment and the wider living world. As designers, we are creative problem-solvers, so the stories we create can be joyful and positive, but they also have to bring something new.'

In a city of competing cultural options, Regent's Park Open Air Theatre offers an experience of nature, creativity and drama combined. It demonstrates how entertainment can rise to environmental challenges, finding new ways to be inspiring and progressive. Here, the landscape is an integral part – and, in some cases, the star – of the show, bringing the audience closer to nature, even as we sit within one of the world's busiest urban metropolises.

'As designers, we are creative problem-solvers, so the stories we create can be joyful and positive, but they also have to bring something new.'

KEN OKONKWO, ARCHITECT AND ASSOCIATE DIRECTOR OF HAWORTH TOMPKINS (PICTURED RIGHT OF IMAGE)

Steve Tompkins (left), director of Haworth Tompkins, with associate director Ken Okonkwo.

The theatre's stage is built out of timber from scratch each year, and sits atop a concrete base which was part of the original 20th-century design.

A play area that imagines a better future

GOLDEN LANE PLAYGROUND, CITY OF LONDON
ARCHITECTS: MUF ARCHITECTURE/ART
BUILT: 2019

At the Golden Lane Estate, between Clerkenwell and the Barbican, muf architecture/art has created a playground of reclaimed, recycled and natural materials for children under the age of five. 'The playground is an essay in materials, encouraging children to have a more intimate relationship with the materiality of the world around them, and start a dialogue about where things come from and how they are made,' says Katherine Clarke, founding member of muf, a collaborative practice of artists, designers and architects who specialise in the design of public spaces.

These are not your standard playground materials. Instead, the 'urban rockery' of textures – old, new, natural, unnatural, polished and raw – reflects and extends the surroundings, allowing children to safely explore their inner-city environment.

The use of stone in the playground is inspired by the rough concrete of the area's Brutalist architecture and the weathered limestone of London Wall, which dates back to the Roman foundations of the city. Stones recovered from local archaeological digs were sourced from a reclamation yard in Shoreditch, while natural sedimentary rocks were sourced from quarries across the UK. These blocks and boulders have been assembled in a rough circle that's perfect for clambering over, jumping off and hiding behind.

Recycled and recyclable materials make up the more traditional elements of the playground: Ecodek, a composite of recycled wood and recycled plastic, is used for the benches; the slide and climbing frame are made from recycled aluminium; and the floor is made from a porous rubber crumb, which absorbs rainwater to alleviate pressure on the drainage system.

As part of the design process, Clarke ran workshops with local children that involved drawing, model-making and observation exercises. 'I think it's important for an adult not to over-determine how a child should play,' she explains. 'Instead, you should think about what kind of experiences you want a child to have. One of our approaches is to design play spaces that feel open-ended or unresolved, so a child can negotiate the landscape of play for themselves.'

A more sustainable London might look quite different to the city we know today, and its creation will depend on future generations. Hopefully, this type of playground design can inspire our children to think about the urban environment in new ways. 'The key to sustainability is to imagine and then inhabit a world that is different to the one we live in now,' says Clarke. 'It's hard to conceptualise change, because everything seems prescribed and pre-meditated on such a large scale, but the city is an interconnected social and environmental web. So, when you can understand and measure, in small ways, the impact of your life on the resources of the city, you can then make proactive choices to influence change.'

'The key to sustainability is to imagine and then inhabit a world that is different to the one we live in now.'

KATHERINE CLARKE, CO-FOUNDER OF MUF ARCHITECTURE/ART (PICTURED BELOW)

Modernising a museum steeped in history

MUSEUM OF THE HOME, HACKNEY
ARCHITECTS: WRIGHT & WRIGHT
COMPLETED: 2021

The Museum of the Home in Hoxton explores how people have lived in the UK throughout history. You can time travel via living spaces, from a parlour in 1695 to a 1990s loft-style apartment, witnessing the impact of technology and globalisation on our homes. The museum's architecture takes visitors on a similar journey: like a miniature city, it is a patchwork of buildings from different eras and personalities.

These include the 300-year-old Geffrye almshouse, a Georgian terrace, a 90s pavilion and even a Victorian pub, the Marquis of Lansdowne. Yet, even though the museum has always been magical, it was, until recently, dysfunctional and slowly deteriorating. In 2010, it was decided that a modern space for collection storage, learning rooms and exhibitions was required. The question was, where should the new building be added?

An easy option would have been to demolish the old pub on the corner, opposite Hoxton Rail Station, to make way for a new, energy-efficient gallery building. Instead, architects Wright & Wright approached the whole site like city planners: re-examining the potential of forgotten spaces. '[Site analysis] is about rooting a project to its place,' explains Naila Yousuf, Senior Architect at Wright & Wright. 'We look at historical area maps to find out what happened in the past, as a building only ever exists because of its place and setting. That is what inevitably grounds a project: the building and context guide you, rather than imposing your ideas on a site.'

The museum's new main entrance, directly opposite Hoxton Station, was originally the back of the site. This revised layout makes the new café and existing garden more accessible to visitors.

OME
MUSEUM OF
THE HOME
REOPENING
SPRING
2021
Museum ↗

The architects' analysis revealed that only one third of the whole museum site was actually being used, and it became clear that 'bringing as much of the Grade I listed building back into use as possible' would be the most sustainable solution. Surprisingly, 80 percent of the reclaimed space was found in the oldest part of the museum, the deteriorating almshouse, which dates back to 1714. Only the raised ground-floor level was being used for exhibition space, as the basement was prone to flooding and the ceiling of the upper level was low: it was in these floors that the architects saw potential. After replacing the crumbling external structure, they dug down and extended up to create two new functional levels.

'There have been radical changes to the building, but Hackney's conservationists were supportive, because the design was about preserving the building long-term and making it more accessible to the public. It was like open heart surgery. Though, when you see it now, you would never know it had happened. For us, that's the success of the project,' says Yousuf.

As well as protecting the heritage for future generations, Wright & Wright preserved the building materials. 'Bricks hold a high amount of embodied carbon, but over the lifecycle of the building the carbon footprint is relatively low, because that carbon dissipates,' Yousuf explains. 'The almshouses have been there for 300 years – and we have preserved them for another 300 years to come.'

They also retrofitted the whole museum: improving insulation, fitting double-glazed windows and upgrading the antiquated services with efficient mechanical systems. These modernisations meant that although two new, single-storey structures – an education studio and lecture room – were added, the site's total energy consumption did not increase.

Just like London itself, the Museum of the Home is a layered, complicated, challenging and fantastic place. It's certainly easier to demolish the past to make way for modernity, but that doesn't mean that it is always the best route. Now, the Marquis of Lansdowne has been transformed into a café and bar for the museum, with a block of flats above, which helped to fund the whole plan. The café is named 'Molly's' after Molly Harrison, an education pioneer who established a school programme at the museum in the 1930s – just one more example of how, by treasuring the past, Wright & Wright makes way for the future.

This area of the 1998 extension by architects Branson Coates was once a café; now, it is a spacious entrance hall that allows the museum to more easily welcome school groups.

MOLLY'S
WELCOM

'The almshouses have been there for 300 years – and we have preserved them for another 300 years to come.'

NAILA YOUSUF, SENIOR ARCHITECT AT WRIGHT & WRIGHT (PICTURED BELOW)

The Standard
Lycamobile
QUICK MOBILE REPAIR
Unlimited
£25

Reinventing a Brutalist icon as a retro hotel

THE STANDARD, KING'S CROSS
ARCHITECTS: ORMS
COMPLETED: 2019

Brutalist architecture in London is divisive. While many love its bold geometry and idealism, an equal number hate its overpowering presence and the failures of said idealism. In King's Cross, one such piece of architecture was up for debate. Completed in 1974 to a design by architect Sydney Cook, the Camden Town Hall Annexe was originally a council office, with a 52-space basement car park. When the offices moved to a new location in 2014, this ailing, clunky building, with its – arguably iconic – round-edged rectangular windows, became redundant. It was an expensive problem waiting to be solved.

In addition to its Brutalist character, the building's value lay in the huge amount of carbon embedded in its concrete structure. As a material, concrete is very carbon-intensive to make. So once it exists, it is more sustainable to try and maximise its use, instead of demolishing it unnecessarily and making new concrete.

Retrofitting is, however, often far more challenging than designing from scratch. This approach requires determined problem-solving at every step. 'If a building is to be successfully retained and repurposed, you need to work with the grain of the building rather than fighting against it,' says Simon Whittaker, architect at Orms. 'You need to recognise which bits need changing and which bits need celebrating.'

Recognising some of the failures of this building as an office block, the architects set about repurposing it into a hotel, which suited the space much better. Imagining a buzzy

’70s-themed hotspot, they proposed a design that would fully embrace the building’s identity, retaining its concrete shell, while bringing it up to 21st-century standards of efficiency.

First, they stripped the building back to its original Brutalist bones. The pre-cast concrete panels that frame the windows were an integral structural element, so could not be altered. However, the original stair core and the level that connected to the neighbouring Camden Town Hall were happily removed. Now, the architects had their canvas to work with.

They designed a three-storey extension to sit atop the existing eight floors, creating the extra space required for the new use of the building as a hotel. The extension is supported by steel columns, which are carefully aligned and threaded through the existing building. It sits atop the colossal concrete building, as a contemporary glass and stainless-steel volume. It’s clear that this addition is a 21st-century one. Yet, the Brutalist geometry of the original structure still serves as its inspiration.

The building was then fitted with technology to help the hotel operate more sustainably on a day-to-day basis. This includes a grey-water recycling system that filters, cleans and reuses water from showers and baths, together with waste water heat-recovery units that use the heat of hot taps to warm the incoming water.

Although 94 percent of the original building was retained, today it has a whole new identity: it is Brutalism 2.0, representing a playful take on the past. A bright red external lift rockets up and down the façade from the street to the 10th-floor rooftop bar. The addition of brick and timber at street level have changed the building’s once hostile relationship with the pedestrian pathway. Tough tropical trees and plants enclose an outdoor seating area, and a neighbouring public garden that was once closed, has been reinstated.

The building now commands a certain status on Euston Road. Just like the Grade I listed St Pancras railway station opposite, designed by Sir George Gilbert Scott, or the British Library on the next corner, designed by Sir Colin St John Wilson, The Standard represents the 1970s history of the city in style. As many late 20th-century buildings reach pivotal moments of survival or demolition, perhaps with a little imagination, they too can be transformed into more sustainable and characterful elements of London’s historic fabric.

‘If a building is to be successfully retained and repurposed, you need to work with the grain of the building rather than fighting against it.’

SIMON WHITTAKER, ARCHITECT AT ORMS
(PICTURED RIGHT OF IMAGE)

John McRae (left) and Simon Whittaker, architects at Orms.

The 266-room hotel includes a bar, recording studio, and three restaurants within the building. Its interiors, which draw inspiration from the '70s, were designed by Archer Humphryes Architects and Shawn Hausman Design.

SOTTSASS

Share

One of the best things cities can offer us is the chance to share resources, knowledge and opportunities with our fellow citizens. Sustainable community spaces, energy hubs and urban farms should form a natural part of a flourishing sustainable city.

A joyful kitchen transforms a disused cottage

HACKNEY SCHOOL OF FOOD, CLAPTON
ARCHITECTS: SURMAN WESTON
COMPLETED: 2020

On the grounds of a Victorian-era school in Clapton, a former caretaker's cottage has been reinvented as the Hackney School of Food – a field-to-fork educational kitchen classroom for local children. Once forgotten, forlorn and unremarkable, today the 1980s building is filled with life: lessons with 30 children happen three times a day; tomatoes, herbs and berries grow in the garden; chickens lay eggs in their hutch; and bees buzz from the beehives to the wildflowers growing in the new orchard.

While the cottage was retained to keep the transformation as cost-efficient as possible, architects Tom Surman and Percy Weston have given it a completely new flavour, creating a practical yet joyful space for learning, cooking and experimenting with food. The former single-storey house is now an airy, double-height classroom, with 10 height-adjustable cooking stations and one teaching station. A new, large rectangular window fills the space with natural light, and provides a view out onto the street and up to the sky for daydreaming.

While the space feels generous and uplifting, its design was a tough exercise in minimalism and restraint. 'Nothing could be superfluous, but that didn't mean that we couldn't be playful,' says Surman. The run-of-the-mill red-brick exterior, for example, is now celebrated – with even more red brick. Outside, the bricks extend to paving, planters and a pizza oven in the kitchen garden; inside, they are referenced with terracotta-coloured tiles and flooring. Once easy to ignore, the red bricks now feel bright and intentional.

For Weston, preserving that patina of the past was important. 'We wanted to expose all the ingredients of the building, so if a child asked about its history, we could point to the upstairs bathroom tiles and tell them it used to be a house.'

The architects really stripped the cottage back to its bones, revealing the structural beams, the roof rafters and everything in between. The walls – whether rough-plastered, block-work, or tiled where the former upstairs bathroom once stood – were left alone and simply painted pale grey. Even more unusually, the roof insulation was left exposed: the architects re-insulated and sealed the roof with spray-foam insulation, and instead of adding cladding, they painted it the same shade of grey, creating a surprisingly dreamy cloud-like effect.

Through simple means, the new design reconnects this building back into the wider ecosystem of the environment and the city. New pipes channel rainwater from the roof into a giant water butt, used for watering the gardens. The eggs from the chickens and the vegetables from the gardens are cooked in the kitchen during lessons. Thanks to its separate entrance from the main school, the cottage can also be rented for out-of-hours events, creating a community space and extra income for the School of Food.

Surman Weston always start by asking the question, how can the use of a building be designed to be sustainable in a broader sense? The Hackney School of Food is a great example of this: even with limited resources, it feeds back productively into the environment, the community and the city. Its creators see it as a prototype for future Schools of Food across London and the UK. Installed into redundant spaces, these schools would teach more children in cities how to live, cook and eat more sustainably, creating a positive ripple effect of sustainable outcomes.

'We wanted to expose all the ingredients of the building, so if a child asked about its history, we could point to the upstairs bathroom tiles and tell them it used to be a house.'

PERCY WESTON, ARCHITECT AND CO-FOUNDER OF SURMAN WESTON (PICTURED RIGHT OF IMAGE)

Tom Surman (left) and Percy Weston, architects and co-founders of Surman Weston.

Tom Walker, Head Food Educator at Hackney School of Food (pictured opposite), picks tomatoes in the productive kitchen garden for his upcoming class. Beyond this kitchen garden, a larger garden features fruit trees, a greenhouse and two beehives, with landscape design by Lidia D'Agostino.

A poignant history meets sustainability

BELARUSIAN MEMORIAL CHAPEL, FINCHLEY
ARCHITECTS: SPHERON ARCHITECTS
BUILT: 2016

This memorial chapel in Finchley was designed for the Belarusian diaspora in London. Inspired by traditional Belarusian wooden churches, the architecture reflects its community's memories with a modern, sustainable timber design. Surrounded by trees, it sets a special atmosphere that is historically significant, carbon-neutral and in harmony with nature.

The chapel sits in the grounds of a community centre that was established in the 1940s, which later became a meeting place for Belarusian people who relocated to the UK after the Second World War, and then a place of worship for Belarusian Greek Catholics. In 2012, the community led by Father Serge decided to commission local resident and architect Tszwai So of Spheron Architects to design their own chapel here.

It was important that the architecture felt authentic, to honour the community's heritage. The chapel is dedicated to the memory of victims of the 1986 Chernobyl nuclear disaster, where thousands of Belarusian people lost their homes, many of which were timber buildings common to rural villages. It is also a place of refuge for Belarusian Greek Catholics, who cannot practice their religion in Belarus today due to political reasons.

The Baroque-style cupola and timber-shingle roof reference the Belarusian Greek Catholic churches of the 18th century, a period before the Greek Catholic denomination was banned in Belarus in 1839, after which these cupolas were gradually replaced with Russian Orthodox onion domes. To design this feature, So combined historical inspiration with contemporary construction techniques. The frame and ribs are made from digitally cut cross-laminated timber, hand-clad with a layer of lead, together with Canadian cedar shingles made by a local carpenter.

The traditional churches were constructed using a log-cabin technique, which involved stacking trunks of larch trees horizontally to form a load-bearing wall. So followed the same method, but adapted it to use cross-laminated timber panels around a structural frame of English Douglas fir. Because the timber pieces were manufactured and prefabricated, the structure took just two days to put together once the material arrived at the site.

Natural light diffuses evenly into the chapel during the day, bringing out the warmth of the timber. Tall frosted windows surround the chapel entrance on the south-facing façade, shaded from unwanted heat by the community centre, while slim, high clerestory windows run the length of the chapel, shaded by the eaves of the roof. Good insulation and an air-source heat pump work together to keep the chapel at an ambient temperature, in addition to ventilation provided via a vent beneath the altar step.

Many Belarusian timber churches no longer survive, because they have been susceptible to fire damage over time. For the same reason, this is the first wooden church built in London since the Great Fire of 1666. Thankfully, cross-laminated timber is much safer to build with as it chars very slowly and predictably, reducing the risk of history repeating itself.

For Tszwai So and his practice, Spheron Architects, when it comes to designing sustainable buildings, the human experience and connection to the architecture is paramount. 'If we manage to save ourselves from extinction to the point where we can start to learn to live with nature in a more responsible and harmonious way, then we will discover that architecture has to go beyond that,' he says.

Inside the 69-square-metre chapel, which seats 40 people, there are wooden memorials, an iconostasis (a screen with historic icons) and traditional white-red-white Belarusian textiles – a national colour combination currently banned in Belarus. The chapel hosts services, choral recitals, poetry readings and memorials for its community.

IC XC
NI KA

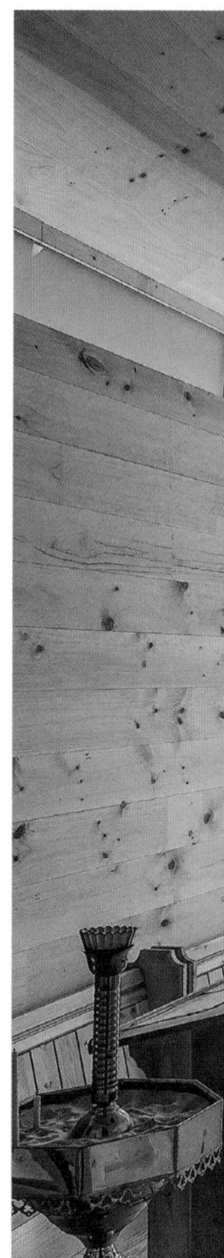

In Belarus, larch is the most available type of wood. To create a similar effect here, architect Tszwai So combined Radiata pine cross-laminated timber panels from Spain, locally sourced English Douglas Fir and Canadian cedar. The tower (pictured above) was constructed using traditional English carpentry techniques, with joints left exposed and pegs extruded.

'We are very interested in people's lived experiences, and their subjective emotional connection with the built environment. This is something we want to pursue on top of the sustainability agenda.'

TSZWAI SO, ARCHITECT AT SPHERON ARCHITECTS (PICTURED OPPOSITE)

Architect Tszwai So (left) with Dr Karalina Matskevich, community member and leader of the Francis Skaryna Belarusian Library and Museum.

A group of nurseries all about reuse

N FAMILY CLUB, VARIOUS LOCATIONS
ARCHITECTS: KENNEDY WOODS
BUILT: 2019–2021

Across London, a series of characterful buildings have been repurposed into a group of neighbourhood nurseries with a sustainable outlook. Sustainability is integral to the N Family Club's business plan and educational curriculum, so when it came to their nursery buildings, it made sense that these values were embedded at every juncture. They commissioned Kennedy Woods, a B-Corp-certified architectural practice, to work on a plan to reimagine each building they found, transforming them into inspiring places for children to learn and play.

The first sustainable step was the decision to reuse existing community buildings, making huge carbon savings and preventing material waste. 'Bringing a new lease of life to an under-loved building will always be more sustainable than tearing it down and starting again,' says Chris Kennedy, architect and co-founder of the practice. 'Finding ways to reimagine those buildings is a rewarding creative challenge.'

The converted buildings include churches, townhouses, care homes and offices. Many were former pillars of the community that had fallen into disrepair, become vacant or required modernisation. At first glance, some seemed tricky to repurpose, yet the team soon found creative uses for the spaces.

For example, a lofty church in Twickenham was divided into smaller spaces with two mezzanines. Meanwhile, the warren-like rooms of a former almshouse in Brixton, which served as an important HIV and AIDs hospice from

> 'Bringing a new lease of life to an under-loved building will always be more sustainable than tearing it down and starting again.'
>
> CHRIS KENNEDY, ARCHITECT AND CO-FOUNDER OF KENNEDY WOODS (PICTURED BELOW)

1989, was opened up to create larger spaces. In other buildings, quirks lent themselves to child-friendly zones, like the pitched-loft conversion in a Georgian townhouse in West Hampstead, which became a perfect den.

Solutions were added to improve energy efficiency throughout, including insulation and double glazing. Air filtration was incorporated via concealed ductwork or standalone units. Outside gardens, at ground-level and on roofs, were created for children to play in. And bicycle and buggy parks were added wherever possible, to encourage parents to cycle or walk.

While each building was unique, the N nurseries required consistent interiors across the whole set. This led Kennedy Woods to devise a design blueprint for calm, uplifting, safe, interactive and healthy learning environments, which could be rolled out over different spaces and used for future expansions. The look employed smooth-plywood joinery, non-toxic, child-friendly materials such as recycled vinyl flooring, and Cradle-to-Cradle certified products, which guarantee circular properties for zero waste.

Taking a broad approach, the N Family Club team also includes environmental thinking in its curriculum: children learn about plastic waste in the ocean; read *Greta and the Giants* (inspired by Thunberg's stand to save the world); practise recycling; develop an understanding of nature by caring for plants, indoor and out; and even add up why taking public transport makes sense in maths. As N Family Club's Chief Strategy Officer, Sarah Mackenzie says: 'We want to unleash a generation of children ready to do good, and our curriculum is designed to build the curiosity, confidence, capability and compassion they need to become informed and inspired change-makers.'

In Twickenham, a former church provided a double-height room that the architects divided with a mezzanine level to create a more functional space for the nursery.

1

In a former townhouse in West Hampstead, a pair of small split-level rooms (pictured above) were opened up and connected with steps that double up as amphitheatre-style seating. While in Stoke Newington, a former art gallery now has a playful new life (pictured opposite, above): the circular window was added by the architects to improve daylight and give the children somewhere to look out onto nature.

At the Brixton (pictured below) and London Fields (pictured opposite) sites, the bespoke playgrounds feature inventive timber structures.

1

A timber canteen makes everyday dining special

IBSTOCK PLACE SCHOOL REFECTORY, ROEHAMPTON
ARCHITECTS: MACCREANOR LAVINGTON
BUILT: 2020

This school dining hall is an homage to the magnificence of timber as a sustainable building material. The naturally ventilated building celebrates communal school life through its large, uplifting interior spaces, where timber plays a leading role. Outside, the building's earth-coloured bricks and red tiles help it settle into the existing campus, which is oriented around an Edwardian manor and a historic orchard.

The new building consists of three soaring pyramidal roofs made from layered 'glulam' (glued laminated timber, sustainably grown and engineered for increased strength), rising to large glazed roof lanterns. The beams are arranged in a lattice of diamonds – a contemporary slant on a traditional cut roof with rafters – with slatted oak panels between them, which also line the lower walls and staircases. All of the timber was cut to length at manufacture, thereby reducing pollution and waste on the construction site.

The use of timber was primarily selected for its carbon-negative properties, but the architects also wanted to play to its strengths as a durable, visually appealing, natural material. 'It looks like a fragile jewel box,' says architect Loretta Gentilini, 'but it's tough – designed to last a long time and age well.' Durability was particularly important, as the building has to carry its school community of four-to-18-year-old pupils from breakfast club at 7am, through a 1,000-person lunch, all the way to evening music recitals and even weddings at the weekend.

Beneath the three roofs, there are a range of different spaces for dining, cooking, gathering and studying. The main dining space shows the majesty of the timber structure to its fullest. The second space is divided horizontally by a mezzanine level, with the kitchen and servery below, and the sixth-form dining room above. The third space holds a quiet sixth-form study room, reached via a discreet door.

Although the building had to be primarily practical, Gentilini attributes its welcoming and uplifting character to the natural and tactile qualities of timber. 'We showed that you can build large interior spaces that also feel warm and connected on a human scale. We exposed the timber as much as possible, because it is a material that has universal appeal and we wanted an interior that people could interact with.'

Due to the heat of the kitchen and the amount of people using the dining room, cooling methods and air ventilation were key to the design. The architects solved both of these 'passively', meaning that there was no need for mechanical air conditioning. Openings in the roof lanterns at the peak of each pyramid provide an exhaust for stale, hot air as it rises. Manually operated vents in the timber panels of the lower walls can be opened to let cool air in.

Windows were carefully positioned to bring in plenty of daylight, without too much heat from the sun. The slim horizontal clerestory windows and roof lanterns allow natural light in for an average of 80 percent of the school day, reducing the need for artificial lighting. Meanwhile, exterior window shutters and a shaded colonnade running alongside the building limit any intense sunlight that might lead to overheating.

This dining hall shows how timber can be used to achieve a truly modern and magical experience of space. Guided by the material's intrinsic qualities, the architecture transforms school dining into a high point of the day, an activity worth cherishing. Perhaps this school refectory should be considered a blueprint for more timber communal buildings that elevate our everyday life in the city.

'We showed that you can build large interior spaces that also feel warm and connected on a human scale.'

LORETTA GENTILINI, ARCHITECT AT MACCREANOR LAVINGTON (PICTURED LEFT OF IMAGE)

Loretta Gentilini (left) and Thomas Ormerod, architects at Maccreanor Lavington.

Preserving an urban forest for future generations

ALEXANDRA ROAD PARK, SOUTH HAMPSTEAD
LANDSCAPE ARCHITECTS: JOHANNA GIBBONS AND NEIL DAVIDSON, J & L GIBBONS
COMPLETED: 2016

Alexandra Road Park is a biodiverse valley between the residential buildings of the Alexandra and Ainsworth Estate in South Hampstead. The 1.7 hectares of linear park were first designed by landscape architect Janet Jack in the 1970s, when the estate was built. Jack's design combined the naturalism of the countryside with the tough requirements of an inner-city park. Sculptural mounds and meadows were planted with hundreds of shrub, hedge and tree species to attract wildlife, while zig-zagging paths created a series of 'outdoor rooms' for basketball and graffiti, parkour and children's play. There's even a grassy amphitheatre with a stage.

'It is a hard-core park, conceived as a piece of the city, to truly serve the city,' says Johanna Gibbons, the landscape architect commissioned to retrofit the park, along with her colleague and fellow landscape architect, Neil Davidson. Originally designed to be tough and low maintenance, the park's drainage systems, seasonality and biodiversity had begun slowly breaking down after its first 45 years in existence. The sloping channels that had been built into the natural landscape for rainwater drainage and irrigation were no longer intact, or had become blocked by leaves. Once evenly spaced trees were now overcrowded, thanks to their self-seeded offspring. The lack of light to the undergrowth had killed off seasonal plants and destroyed many habitats for wildlife, such as foraging birds.

Gibbons and Davidson conducted careful research, before coming up with a plan to equip the park for another 40 years, which included reinstalling the original systems, conducting planned tree surgery and planting new species. There are now 130 trees in the forest, including over 25 species, ranging from birch trees, which are native to the UK, to more exotic varieties, such as Eucalyptus, native to Australia and Tasmania. The landscape architect duo examined the list of plants included in the original design to assess those which hadn't survived and which species might be more resilient to the changing climate.

'It was essential management,' says Gibbons. 'In the elongated woodland, the trees were stretching to find light. Targeted removals brought light down to the ground, to wild flowers, bulbs and shrubs. Then, we replanted to bring back seasonality and structure, creating glades in this urban forest. Photos from the late '70s show small trees that 40 years later are huge, demonstrating how quickly landscapes evolve. Change is part of that landscape. So, we design with time, anticipating what something will look like in 50 and 100 years.'

Future-proofing the park was an important part of the design. 'One of the biggest challenges in cities will be the increasing frequency of extreme weather events,' explains Davidson. 'Flooding is likely to become more prevalent, so whatever we can do to keep water "local" and allow it to drain over time is important.' In response to this issue, the architects carefully reinstated the original low-tech water drainage trenches, backfilled with gravel and sand, and unblocked some of the concrete channels that lead into them. 'It was a tricky and delicate job, often working by hand so as not to disturb the growth of existing plants and trees,' Davidson continues. In addition to this, some paths were restored with fine gravel, a porous surface that allows water to drain into the ground.

Another key issue critical to the retrofit was ecological justice, important in a densely built-up city such as London, where nature must be shared. Ecological justice is about everyone having a right to participate in and access nature – a challenge to which there isn't necessarily one direct solution, especially when there are many different groups of people living side by side. The landscaping design process, therefore, must draw together lots of solutions to suit the community, and build local skills and knowledge to enable people who live and work in the area to look after their landscapes.

'Taking care of what you have made: that is the tricky part of landscape architecture,' says Davidson. 'Our approach to designing sustainable cities always returns to that idea: how can we look after these landscapes we have created for future generations? How can we allow them to thrive and be nurtured, to equip them for the long term?'

Beyond its large parks, London is known for its pockets of green space, which support the surrounding urban communities, from the squares of Bloomsbury and Kensington, to Modernist visions of landscapes, such as Alexandra Road Park. As lifelines for relaxation, play, exercise and health, their upkeep comes with a great responsibility. Whereas in architecture the term 'retrofit' might be more synonymous with buildings, the work at Alexandra Road Park shows how green spaces, too, must be carefully maintained and cared for, to continue to foster the sustainability of the city.

‘Sustainability is about preserving those fundamental resources that we need to survive – food, water, soil and oxygen, which are all linked to the health of our landscapes. You can start on a planetary scale, then adjust it to the scale of London.’

NEIL DAVIDSON, LANDSCAPE ARCHITECT AND PARTNER AT J & L GIBBONS (PICTURED RIGHT OF IMAGE)

Landscape architects Johanna Gibbons and Neil Davidson (pictured opposite) designed the planting around the retrofitted park to be low-maintenance and self-sufficient.

PHOENIX

A slice of wild nature in the West End

PHOENIX GARDEN COMMUNITY BUILDING, COVENT GARDEN
ARCHITECTS: OFFICE SIAN ARCHITECTURE + DESIGN
BUILT: 2017

The Phoenix Garden is a hidden oasis of wildlife a stone's throw from London's Covent Garden. Well-used as a lunchtime escape by office workers and frequented by birds seeking a green perch, the garden has a long history of resilience. It opened in 1984 on the site of a former WWII bombing. Originally, it was one of seven community gardens located around the West End, but today, sadly, it is the only one that remains.

To ensure its place in the city, Gurmeet Sian, architect and founder of Office Sian, designed a simple and flexible building to support the activities of the garden, inspired by its ethos of nurturing sustainability and community. The brick, limestone and timber building with a green roof holds a simple multi-purpose space for events, workshops and parties, plus a small kitchen with a hatch for serving tea and coffee, toilets and an office. An important base for the garden's volunteers and visitors, it also brings in useful revenue for the charity.

Inspired by traditional English walled gardens, Sian liked the idea of using the architecture to form a protective shell for nature, guarding it from the surrounding roads and tall buildings. Capped with limestone, the exterior brick wall of the building forms a tough new corner on the edge of the garden, while the arched timber doorway and tree tops that peep over the wall give passers-by a hint of the magical oasis within.

Stepping inside, the building transforms from a protective fortress into an airy garden pavilion filled with daylight. In contrast to the armour-like exterior, the opposite façade of the building is porous, featuring a curved wall of glazing that can be folded right back, with timber cladding that reflects the soft natural setting of the garden. Blurring the boundaries between indoors and out, the architecture draws visitors into the garden, while bringing its green views inside.

To create a practical and utilitarian interior, Sian used durable and low-maintenance materials, which have been left exposed. Timber plywood panels line the ceiling and neatly conceal storage and the kitchen hatch. Thick, tactile wooden pillars support the roof of the building. And the brick flooring connects with the pathways of the garden, built using old bricks found on the site by the gardener and volunteers.

The Phoenix Garden community building encourages a human connection to wildness in the heart of the city, where it has often been lost. Though modest and simple in its design, this building is powerful in its proposition to protect and sustain the natural habitat, its urban community of wildlife and garden lovers alike.

'This building and garden sits in one of the busiest commercial districts in the world. We shoehorned in as many sustainable features as possible, and the close connection between building and garden was very important.'

GURMEET SIAN, ARCHITECT AND FOUNDER OF OFFICE SIAN (PICTURED OPPOSITE)

After such a collaborative and rewarding design process, architect Gurmeet Sian (pictured above) developed a real emotional attachment to the building. In fact, he even hosted his wedding breakfast in the garden.

A community building using recycled materials

SANDS END ARTS AND COMMUNITY CENTRE, FULHAM
ARCHITECTS: MAE ARCHITECTS
BUILT: 2021

Welcome to South Park in Fulham. If you're reaching the park from Parsons Green Station, you'll be greeted by this beautiful community centre, positioned like a gate-house on the corner. Commissioned by the London Borough of Hammersmith & Fulham Council, the building is a functional piece of the urban park, providing vital facilities such as a café and toilets, plus rooms for events that complement the outdoor sports activities held here.

Designed by Mae Architects, the community centre has been built using over 35 percent recycled materials. It is clad with bricks that have been upcycled from over 28 tonnes of construction waste, which would typically go into landfill. The architects worked with specialist Dutch brick manufacturers StoneCycling, and the bricks were laid on their sides to reduce the number needed by 60 percent.

The sustainably sourced, cross-laminated timber structure, designed in collaboration with engineering practice Elliott Wood, dramatically reduced the embodied carbon of the building. The frame was bolted together, instead of glued, for ease of future disassembly and reuse. Then, because the timber was fairly lightweight, the concrete slabs could be thinned to just 1.75cm in depth, reducing the amount of concrete needed. Inside, the timber has been left exposed and stained green for an interior finish that subtly nods to nature.

The new centre connects to an existing gatekeeper's lodge, which dates back to 1903.

'There are challenges and hurdles with every project, but there always has to be an opportunity, however small, to be exemplary and to change architecture and construction for the better.'

MICHAEL DILLON, ARCHITECT AT MAE ARCHITECTS (PICTURED BELOW)

The old lodge had fallen into disrepair after 40 years of unoccupancy, but has now been refurbished as an important element of the community complex. Today, it appears completely transformed, as a double-height arts space with useful mezzanine storage. It's surprising how well the modern building and the old lodge complement each other, forming a practical, L-shaped, gate-keeping hybrid.

As well as being built with recycled, sustainable and existing materials that all contribute to carbon savings, the buildings help their urban community to sustain a connection to the green space. The natural meeting place draws locals in, with its multi-purpose hall and common room that's designed for everything from weekly dance classes to weddings, coffee mornings and clubs. It is a useful piece of park infrastructure, encouraging people to linger for longer and to really enjoy their time in the urban outdoors.

30

An eco energy centre that's a local landmark

BUNHILL 2 ENERGY CENTRE, ISLINGTON
ARCHITECTS: CULLINAN STUDIO
BUILT: 2020

Walking up City Road from Old Street to Angel, a large monolithic box clad in perforated panels might catch your eye. It is an intriguing piece of architecture – and one that's crucially missing a door. This is a building for energy, rather than people. Commissioned by Islington Council, Bunhill 2 Energy Centre is the first of its kind in London, and in Europe. It captures waste heat from the Tube, and converts it into energy to heat 1,350 homes and a leisure centre in the local area.

If Bunhill 2 Energy Centre isn't a building that hosts the community, it does immediately serve it through its purpose. As part of a 'district heat network', the centre acts like a large boiler, directing heat through insulated pipes to heat exchangers inside each home. It's more energy-efficient than having gas boilers in every home and it's flexible to receiving energy converted from waste or renewable sources.

Adopting a more circular approach is important for cities looking to use less energy and become less polluted. For the most efficient solution, centres that convert energy must be placed close to the source of the waste product. For example, on City Road, waste heat was being pumped out of a Northern Line Tube vent at 18 to 28 degrees celsius: today, Bunhill 2 sits atop that vent, making good use of it. In the future, energy centres like this might characterise more of London's neighbourhoods, so it's important to consider their aesthetic.

As tall as a four-storey building, Bunhill 2 is a prominent structure, equivalent to the size of

‘We wanted to take the opportunity to make Bunhill 2 more than the sum of its parts – to look at the long views, the short views, the tactility, the quality, the colours.’

ALEX ABBEY, ARCHITECT AND PARTNER AT CULLINAN STUDIO (PICTURED LEFT OF IMAGE)

other large-scale public architecture. The challenge for Islington-based architects Cullinan Studio was deciding what this new piece of green technology should look like. First, they researched London’s history of innovation and infrastructure design, from Joseph Bazalgette’s sewerage system and its ornate pumping stations to Sir Giles Gilbert Scott’s bright red phone boxes, and Edward Johnston’s typography and graphics for the Tube.

The architects saw an exciting opportunity to contribute to this history, and aimed to bring the same sense of humanity, joy and curiosity to their design. ‘The site was once a miserable no-man’s land. We wanted to design something about the city and for the city,’ says architect Alex Abbey. ‘One aspect of the design is about understanding a new technology and working out how to make the guts of it work. But we also wanted to take the opportunity to make Bunhill 2 more than the sum of its parts: to look at the long views, the short views, the tactility, the quality, the colours – even asking, what will it look like in autumn against the leaves? We pulled all these strands together to place it within a much bigger picture.’

The façade of the energy centre is made of rusty red, copper-clad aluminium panels, a colour chosen as a soft nod to the Northern Line’s oxblood tiles. The panels are perforated with a pattern that is based upon the movement of hot air rising, which was sketched by architect Carol Costello on a Tube journey. The enamelled-steel base of the building features a tessellating cast-aluminium artwork, inspired by the design of local estates by artist Toby Paterson. For Costello, these decorative references bring ‘emotional durability’ to the design, an approach that encourages longevity through forging an attachment to the local community.

‘To be truly sustainable, a building has to have value and people have to value it – otherwise it is a complete waste of resources,’ says Abbey. ‘We have been designing low-energy buildings for a long time. We know how to do it, and work with the best engineers to get there. But, a building has to have delight in order to be sustainable. It has to stimulate contact with humans: people have to enjoy using it, or being in it.’

As technology is always in development, the prefabricated steel structure has been designed to be fully demountable, so it can be easily updated, or to enable all of its parts and materials to be reused or recycled. After all, this energy centre represents just a small piece in a much bigger puzzle of how London will reach net zero – a puzzle that is yet to be designed. Could compact and colourful energy centres become as ubiquitous (and iconic) as phone boxes once were?

Architects Alex Abbey (left) and Carol Costello of Cullinan Studio.

NOVO

An agricultural eden among the skyscrapers

SURREY DOCKS CITY FARM, ROTHERHITHE
ARCHITECTS: PUP ARCHITECTS
COMPLETED: 2020

This working farm was first established in 1975 on a swathe of wasteland in the Docklands, before moving to its current 2.2-acre site in 1986. A slice of agricultural countryside on the edge of the Thames, it sits in polar opposition to the towers of Canary Wharf on the other side of the river. Over the years, the farm has grown into a lively and indispensable community hub that hosts classes and workshops, and is a popular weekend destination for Londoners who stop by for a coffee, or to pick up some farm produce.

The late '80s saw a little complex of tough, utilitarian buildings spring up to support the activities of the farm: firstly, a low-rise black timber structure with a green roof, later followed by a compact three-storey block-work 'tower', with an adjoining pitched-roof outbuilding. After the tower was damaged by a fire and fell into dereliction, the farm called on Chloë Leen and Theo Molloy of PUP Architects to recover the building and return its vital space for offices and classrooms back to the farm.

Inspired by the utilitarian spirit of the site, the architects devised a practical and sustainable plan to retrofit the tower and add a small extension using raw and robust natural materials. 'As a charity that specialises in the environment and sustainable animal husbandry, the farm wanted a building that would reflect its values and explain ideas of sustainability to people who visited,' says Molloy.

Instead of demolishing the tower, materials were layered on top of the existing block-work

> 'The farm wanted a building that would reflect its values and explain ideas of sustainability to people who visited.'
>
> THEO MOLLOY, ARCHITECT AND CO-DIRECTOR OF PUP ARCHITECTS

structure. First, it was wrapped externally with insulation, then double-glazed windows and high-performance doors were added, and rough-sawn timber cladding produced the final layer. The timber was chosen not only for its sustainable credentials as a carbon-negative material, but also for its reference to the site's history as a timber wharf and shipyard. Its black colour nods to the old tar-painted barns of Sussex and Kent. PUP's design has transformed the damp, derelict and uninsulated tower into a warm and modern building that requires minimal heating.

'Though it is a practical design, it doesn't mean it wasn't very thoughtfully considered,' says Molloy. 'A lot of work went into thinking about the quality of the space, the proportions, the light and the detailing.' One such detail is a stained-glass window made by a farm volunteer, which the architects carefully removed and refitted into the new design. Another is the weathervane, specially designed for the farm and based on their Oxford Sandy and Black rare-breed pigs.

A new timber-framed extension to the tower has a saw-tooth-shaped roof, and large glass windows and doors that open up the farm to the Thames path, which is frequented by local runners, dog-walkers and families. Wildflowers and tomatoes grow around a seating area and patio, which was built with granite blocks reclaimed from elsewhere on the farm, together with leftover bricks from a nearby car park.

For PUP, sustainable design is not necessarily a grand statement; it is a series of clever decisions, each made to reduce the environmental impact of a building. 'Sustainability is about seeing architecture as part of a much wider system,' says Molloy. 'It reaches back to the economies you support by the materials you choose, forward to the daily energy use and efficiency, and then to the end of its life when those materials can be reused or recycled. All of your design decisions affect the system.'

The Farm brings together gardens, orchards, food production, livestock rearing, a café and a farm shop. The interiors feature a simple material palette of timber window frames and built-in furniture, against exposed trusses and ceiling joists.

The refurbishment and extension project designed by Chloë Leen (pictured left of image) and Theo Molloy of PUP Architects opened up the farm to the riverside with a new public entrance, a café and a wildflower-filled garden.

Harriet Thorpe is a journalist, writer and editor based in London. After cutting her teeth on the architecture desk at the world's leading design magazine, *Wallpaper**, she decided to tighten her focus to writing about sustainable architecture in her home city. When not at her desk, Harriet loves zooming around east London on her bike in the sunshine and swimming at the epic, Zaha Hadid-designed Olympic pool.

Taran Wilkhu is a British Indian lifestyle photographer specialising in interiors, architecture and portraits. He was born in Yorkshire, but currently resides in a timber-framed house designed by Walter Segal in south east London (which you might just recognise from p.70). Taran had multiple career pivots (from teaching to travel, and from film to finance) before finding his true calling as a photographer. His work has now been featured in publications ranging from *AD* to *Vogue Living*, *Elle Decoration* and *Architects' Journal*, as well as in another of Hoxton Mini Press's books: *An Opinionated Guide to London Architecture*.

Hoxton Mini Press is a small, east London publisher, run by a handful of book-mad people and two dogs, Bug and Moose. We are dedicated to making books that tell fascinating stories through great photography and passionate writing. We think that, in a digital world, the printed book is a special object, but we also believe in giving back a little of what we take: we offset all of the emissions from our production and printing and, for every book you buy from our website, we plant a tree.

Photographer Taran Wilkhu and author Harriet Thorpe, meeting the residents of Hackney School of Food (p.182).

The Sustainable City
First edition

Published in 2022 by Hoxton Mini Press, London.

Text © Harriet Thorpe, photography © Taran Wilkhu*, design by Tom Etherington, assistant photography post-production by Rohit Kalyane, project-editing by Florence Filose, copy-editing by Farah Shafiq, proofreading by Colette Meacher, production by Anna De Pascale and Sarah-Louise Deazley, production support by Becca Jones.

*Except for: both Murray Grove images on p.41 © Will Pryce;
Regent's Park Open Air Theatre image on p.156 © Philip Vile / Haworth Tompkins;
Regent's Park Open Air Theatre image on pp.160–1 © David Jensen;
Museum of the Home image on pp.168–9 © Hufton+Crow;
photo of the authors on p.238 © Felix Hall Close.

Taran: Thanks to all who contributed to this book, including architecture comms expert Celeste Bolte, who introduced me to my partner-in-crime, Harriet, and suggested we work together. Also, a special mention to my wife, Celine, and boys, Sohan and Nayan, who constantly inspire and believe in me, you make me so proud.

Harriet: Thank you to everyone who contributed to this book, and special thanks to Celeste Bolte, Sujata Burman, Thomas Howells, Francesca Perry, Architects Climate Action Network, and Jane and Christopher Thorpe for inspiration, love and support.

 A CIP catalogue record for this book is available from the British Library.

ISBN: 978-1-914314-18-6

Printed and bound by FINIDR, Czech Republic

Hoxton Mini Press is an environmentally conscious publisher, committed to offsetting our carbon footprint. This book is 100% carbon compensated, with offset purchased from Stand For Trees.

For every book you buy from our website, we plant a tree:
www.hoxtonminipress.com